SPANISH
in 10 minutes a day®

by **Kristine K. Kershul, M.A., University of California, Santa Barbara**

Consultant: **Carrie R. Tamburo, Ph. D.**

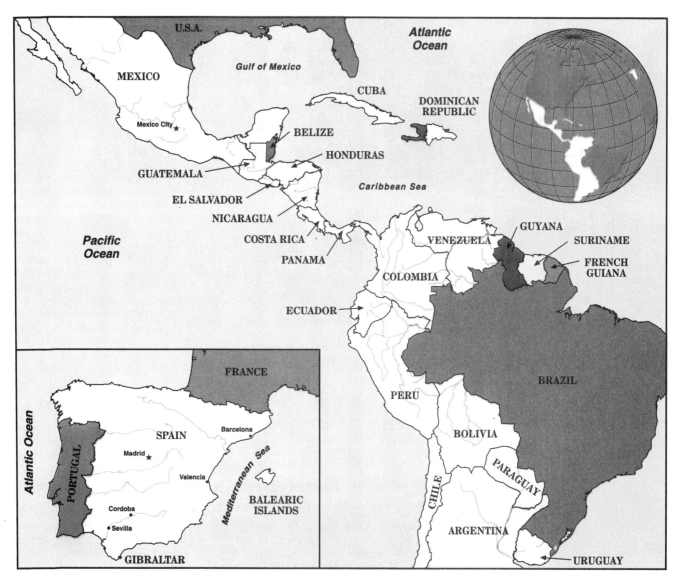

Bilingual Books, Inc.

1719 West Nickerson Street, Seattle, WA 98119
Tel: (206) 284-4211 Fax: (206) 284-3660
www.bbks.com • www.10minutesaday.com

ISBN-13: 978-1-931873-11-6   First printing, October 2007

Can you say this?

(keh)   *(es)*   *(eh-soh)*
¿Qué es eso?
what   is   that

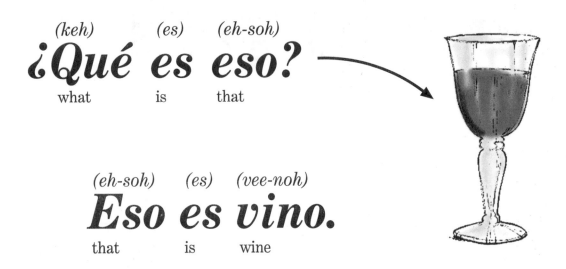

(eh-soh)   *(es)*   *(vee-noh)*
Eso es vino.
that   is   wine

(yoh)   *(kee-yeh-roh)*   *(oon)*   *(vah-soh)*   *(deh)*   *(vee-noh)*
Yo quiero un vaso de vino.
I   want/would like   a   glass   of   wine

If you can say this, you can learn to speak Spanish. You will be able to easily order wine, lunch, theater tickets, pastry, or anything else you wish. You simply ask **"¿Qué es eso?"** *(keh) (es) (eh-soh)* and, upon learning what it is, you can order it with **"Yo quiero eso"** *(yoh) (kee-yeh-roh) (eh-soh)*. Sounds easy, doesn't it?

The purpose of this book is to give you an **immediate** speaking ability in Spanish. Spanish is the leading language in not only Spain and Mexico, but throughout Central and South America. Spanish is a language which is very easy to pronounce. To aid you this book offers a unique and easy system of pronunciation above each word which walks you through learning Spanish.

If you are planning a trip or moving to where Spanish is spoken, you will be leaps ahead of everyone if you take just a few minutes a day to learn the easy key words that this book offers. Start with Step 1 and don't skip around. Each day work as far as you can comfortably go in those 10 minutes. Don't overdo it. Some days you might want to just review. If you forget a word, you can always look it up in the glossary. Spend your first 10 minutes studying the map on the previous page. And yes, have fun learning your new language.

As you work through the Steps, always use the special features which only this series offers. You have sticky labels and flash cards, free words, puzzles, and quizzes. When you have completed the book, cut out the menu guide and take it along on your trip.

1 El Alfabeto

(el) *(ahl-fah-beh-toh)*
the alphabet

Above all new words is an easy pronunciation guide. Refer to this Step whenever you need help, but remember, spend no longer than 10 minutes a day.

Most letters in Spanish are identical to those in English. Many Spanish letters are pronounced just as they are in English, however, others are pronounced quite differently.

To learn the sounds of the Spanish letters, here is the entire alphabet. Practice these sounds with the examples given which are mostly Spanish first names. You can always refer back to these pages if you need to review.

Spanish letter	English sound	Examples	Write it here
a	ah	**Ana** *(ah-nah)*	
ai	i/y	**Jaime** *(hi-meh)*	
au	ow	**Augusto** *(ow-goos-toh)*	
b	b	**Beatriz** *(beh-ah-trees)*	
c	*(before e or i)* s	**Graciela** *(grah-see-eh-lah)*	
	(elsewhere) k	**Carlos** *(kar-lohs)*	Carlos, Carlos, Carlos
ch	ch	**Archibaldo** *(ar-chee-bahl-doh)*	
d	d	**David** *(dah-veed)*	
e	*(as in let)* eh	**Elena** *(eh-leh-nah)*	
ei	*(as in day)* ay	**Reinaldo** *(ray-nahl-doh)*	
er	air	**Fernando** *(fair-nahn-doh)*	
eu	eh-oo	**Eugenio** *(eh-oo-hen-ee-oh)*	
f	f	**Federico** *(feh-deh-ree-koh)*	
g	*(before e or i)* h	**Geofredo** *(heh-oh-freh-doh)*	
	(elsewhere) g	**Gregorio** *(greh-gor-ee-oh)*	
h	silent	**Hugo** *(oo-goh)*	
i	ee	**Isabel** *(ees-ah-bel)*	
j	h	**José** *(hoh-seh)*	
k	k	**Kenia** *(ken-ee-ah)* Kenya	

Letter	Sound	Example	Write it here
l	l	**L**ucas (*loo-kahs*)	
ll	y	Gui**ll**ermo (*gee-yair-moh*)	
m	m	**M**aría (*mah-ree-ah*)	
n	n	**N**icolás (*nee-koh-lahs*)	
ñ	(as in canyon) n-y	Espa**ñ**a (*es-pahn-yah*) Spain	
o	oh	**O**livia (*oh-lee-vee-ah*)	
oi oy	oy	M**oi**sés (*moy-ses*)	
p	p	**P**edro (*peh-droh*)	
q*	k	**Q**uintín (*keen-teen*)	
r	(slightly rolled) r	**R**osa (*roh-sah*)	
rr	(heavily rolled) rr	Inglate**rr**a (*een-glah-teh-rrah*) England	
s	s	**S**amuel (*sah-moo-el*)	Samuel, Samuel
t	t	**T**omás (*toh-mahs*)	
u	oo	**U**rbano (*oor-bah-noh*)	
ua	wah	G**ua**lterio (*gwahl-tair-ee-oh*)	
ue	weh	Man**ue**la (*mah-nweh-lah*)	
v	v	**V**icente (*vee-sen-teh*)	
w	v	**W**ashington (*vah-sheeng-tohn*)	
x	k-s/s	Ma**x**imiliano (*mahk-see-mee-lee-ah-noh*)	
y	y/ee	Nueva **Y**ork (*nweh-vah*)(*york*) New	
z	s	**Z**acarías (*sah-kah-ree-ahs*)	

Just as in English, "q" is always joined with the letter "u." The letter "u" is silent.

Don't worry about whether or not you roll your "r's" perfectly. What is important, is to learn as many words as possible so that you can put them together in sentences and communicate!

Sometimes the phonetics may seem to contradict your pronunciation guide. Don't panic! The easiest and best possible phonetics have been chosen for each individual word. Pronounce the phonetics just as you see them. Don't over-analyze them. Speak with a Spanish accent and, above all, enjoy yourself!

When you arrive in **México,** *(meh-hee-koh)* **España** *(es-pahn-yah)* Spain or another Spanish-speaking country, the very first thing you will need to do is ask questions — "Where (**dónde**) *(dohn-deh)* is the bus stop?" "**Dónde** *(dohn-deh)* where can I exchange money?" "**Dónde** *(dohn-deh)* is the lavatory?" "**Dónde** *(dohn-deh)* is a restaurant?" "**Dónde** *(dohn-deh)* do I catch a taxi?" "**Dónde** is a good hotel?" where "**Dónde** is my luggage?" where — and the list will go on and on for the entire length of your visit. In Spanish, there are SEVEN KEY QUESTION WORDS to learn. For example, the seven key question words will help you find out exactly what you are ordering in a restaurant before you order it — and not after the surprise (or shock!) arrives. Notice that only one letter is different in the Spanish words for "when" and "how much." Don't confuse them! Take a few minutes to study and practice saying the seven key question words listed below. Then cover the Spanish with your hand and fill in each of the blanks with the matching Spanish **palabra.** *(pah-lah-brah)* word

(dohn-deh)
DÓNDE   =   WHERE   _dónde, dónde, dónde_

(keh)
QUÉ   =   WHAT _____

(kee-en)
QUIÉN   =   WHO _____

(por) *(keh)*
POR QUÉ   =   WHY _____

(kwahn-doh)
CUÁNDO   =   WHEN _____

(koh-moh)
CÓMO   =   HOW _____

(kwahn-toh)
CUÁNTO   =   HOW MUCH _____

Now test yourself to see if you really can keep these **palabras** *(pah-lah-brahs)* straight in your mind. Draw lines between the Spanish **y** *(ee)* English equivalents below.

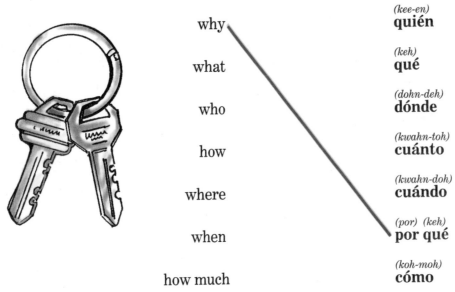

why	**quién** *(kee-en)*
what	**qué** *(keh)*
who	**dónde** *(dohn-deh)*
how	**cuánto** *(kwahn-toh)*
where	**cuándo** *(kwahn-doh)*
when	**por qué** *(por) (keh)*
how much	**cómo** *(koh-moh)*

Examine the following questions containing these **palabras** *(pah-lah-brahs)*. Practice the sentences out loud **y** *(ee)* then practice by copying the Spanish in the blanks underneath each question.

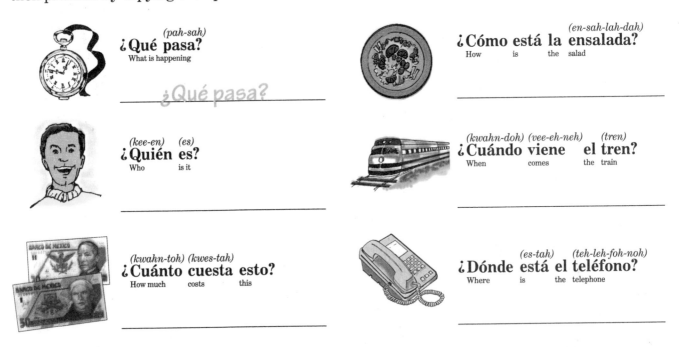

¿**Qué** **pasa?** *(pah-sah)*
What is happening

¿Qué pasa?

¿**Cómo** está la **ensalada?** *(en-sah-lah-dah)*
How   is   the   salad

_____

¿**Quién** **es?** *(kee-en) (es)*
Who   is it

_____

¿**Cuándo** **viene** el **tren?** *(kwahn-doh) (vee-eh-neh) (tren)*
When   comes   the   train

_____

¿**Cuánto** **cuesta** esto? *(kwahn-toh) (kwes-tah)*
How much   costs   this

_____

¿**Dónde** está el **teléfono?** *(es-tah) (teh-leh-foh-noh)*
Where   is   the   telephone

_____

"**Dónde**" *(dohn-deh)* will be your most used question **palabra.** Say each of the following Spanish sentences aloud. Then write out each sentence without looking at the example. If you don't succeed on the first try, don't give up. Just practice each sentence until you are able to do it easily. Remember "**ei**" is pronounced like "ay" in "day" **y** *(ee)* "**ie**" is pronounced "ee-eh."

¿Dónde están los servicios?
(es-tahn) *(sair-vee-see-ohs)*
Where   are   the   restrooms

¿Dónde está el taxi?
(es-tah) *(tahk-see)*
Where   is   taxi

¿Dónde está el autobús?
(ow-toh-boos)
Where   is   bus

_____

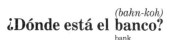
¿Dónde está el taxi?

_____

¿Dónde está el restaurante?
(res-tow-rahn-teh)
restaurant

¿Dónde está el banco?
(bahn-koh)
bank

¿Dónde está el hotel?
(oh-tel)
hotel

_____   _____   _____

Sí, you can see similarities between **inglés** and **español** if you look closely. You will be amazed
(see)   *(een-gles)*   *(es-pahn-yohl)*
yes   English   Spanish

at the number of **palabras** which are identical (or almost identical) in both languages. Of course,
(pah-lah-brahs)
words

they do not always sound the same when spoken by a Spanish-speaking person, but the similarities

will certainly surprise you **y** make your work here easier. Listed below are five "free" **palabras**
(ee)

beginning with "**a**" to help you get started. Be sure to say each **palabra** aloud **y** then write out
(ah)   *(ee)*

the Spanish **palabra** in the blank to the right.
(pah-lah-brah)

☑	**abril** *(ah-breel)*	April		_abril, abril, abril, abril, abril_
☐	**absoluto** *(ahb-soh-loo-toh)*	absolute		_____
☐	**el accidente** *(ahk-see-den-teh)*	accident	**a**	_____
☐	**activo** *(ahk-tee-voh)*	active		_____
☐	**el acto** *(ahk-toh)*	act (of a play)		_____

Free **palabras** like these will appear at the bottom of the following pages in a yellow color band.

They are easy — enjoy them! Remember, in Spanish, the letter "**h**" **es** silent.
(es)
is

(es-pahn-yohl)
Español has multiple **palabras** for "the" and "a," but they are very easy. If the Spanish word
Spanish   words

ends in "**a**" (feminine) it *usually* will have the article "**la**" or "**una**." If the word ends in "**o**"

(masculine) it *usually* will have the article "**el**" or "**un**."

(el) (neen-yoh)
el niño
the   boy

(lohs) (neen-yohs)
los niños
the   boys

(lah) (neen-yah)
la niña
the   girl

(lahs) (neen-yahs)
las niñas
the   girls

(tren)
el tren
the   train

(tren-es)
los trenes
the   trains

(oon-ah) (pah-lah-brah)
una palabra
a   word

(oon-ahs)
unas palabras
some   words

(oon-ah) (ah-meh-ree-kah-nah)
una americana
an   American (female)

(oon-ahs) (ah-meh-ree-kah-nahs)
unas americanas
some   Americans (female)

(oon) (ah-meh-ree-kah-noh)
un americano
an   American (male)

(oon-ohs) (ah-meh-ree-kah-nohs)
unos americanos
some   Americans (male or mixed)

(een-gles)
This might appear difficult, but only because it is different from **inglés.** Just remember you will

be understood whether you say "**la palabra**" or "**el palabra**." Soon you will automatically select

the right article without even thinking about it.

In Step 2 you were introduced to the Seven Key
QuestionWords. These seven words are the basics, the
most essential building blocks for learning Spanish.
Throughout this book you will come across keys
asking you to fill in the missing question word. Use
this opportunity not only to fill in the blank on that
key, but to review all your question words. Play with
the new sounds, speak slowly and have fun.

☐ **agosto** *(ah-gohs-toh)* . . . . August
☐ **la agricultura** *(ah-gree-kool-too-rah)* . . . . agriculture
☐ **el álgebra** *(ahl-heh-brah)* . . . . algebra   **a**
☐ **América** *(ah-meh-ree-kah)* . . . . America
☐ **el animal** *(ah-nee-mahl)* . . . . animal

Before you proceed with this Step, situate yourself comfortably in your living room. Now look

around you. Can you name the things that you see in this **cuarto** *(kwar-toh)* in Spanish? You can probably

guess **la lámpara** *(lahm-pah-rah)* and maybe even **el sofá.** *(soh-fah)* Let's learn the rest of them. After practicing

these **palabras** out loud, write them in the blanks below.

(ven-tah-nah)
la ventana
window
_____

la lámpara *(lahm-pah-rah)* _____
lamp

el sofá *(soh-fah)* _____
sofa

la silla *(see-yah)* _____
chair

la alfombra *(ahl-fohm-brah)* _____
carpet

la mesa *(meh-sah)* _____la mesa, la mesa_____
table

la puerta *(pwair-tah)* _____
door

el reloj *(reh-loh)* _____
clock

la cortina *(kor-tee-nah)* _____
curtain

el teléfono *(teh-leh-foh-noh)* _____
telephone

(peen-too-rah)
la pintura
picture
_____

You will notice that the correct form of **el** or **la** is given **con** *(kohn)* each noun. This tells you whether the

noun is masculine (**el**) or feminine (**la**). Now open your **libro** *(lee-broh)* to the sticky labels on page 17 and

later on page 35. Peel off the first 11 labels **y** proceed around **el cuarto,** *(kwar-toh)* labeling these items in

your home. This will help to increase your **palabra en español** power easily. Don't forget to say
word   Spanish

each **palabra** as you attach the label.

Now ask yourself, "**¿Dónde está la lámpara?**" *(lahm-pah-rah)* **y** point at it while you answer, "**Allí** *(ah-yee)* **está**
there   is

la lámpara." Continue on down the list above until you feel comfortable with these new **palabras.**

❏ **anual** *(ah-noo-ahl)*	annual	_____
❏ **la aplicación** *(ah-plee-kah-see-ohn)*	application	_____
❏ **el artista** *(ar-tees-tah)*	artist	**a** _____
❏ **la atención** *(ah-ten-see-ohn)*	attention	_____
❏ **el automóvil** *(ow-toh-moh-veel)*	auto, car	_____

9

(kah-sah)
la casa = the house

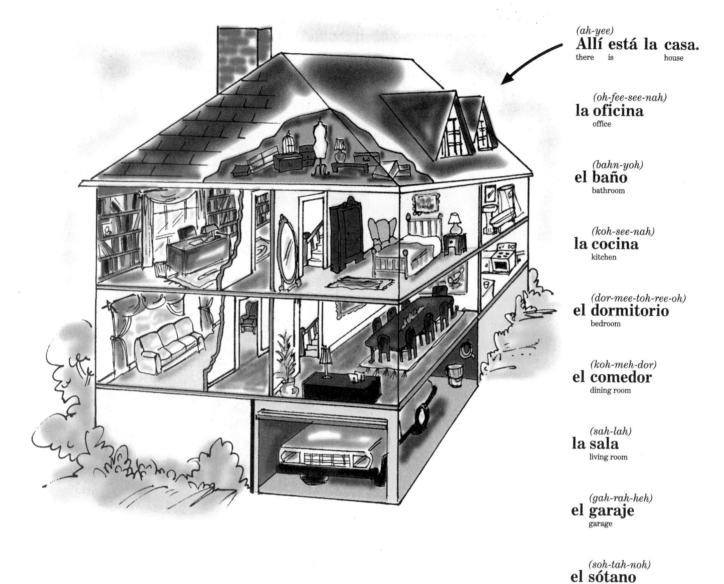

(ah-yee)
Allí está la casa.
there   is   house

(oh-fee-see-nah)
la oficina
office

(bahn-yoh)
el baño
bathroom

(koh-see-nah)
la cocina
kitchen

(dor-mee-toh-ree-oh)
el dormitorio
bedroom

(koh-meh-dor)
el comedor
dining room

(sah-lah)
la sala
living room

(gah-rah-heh)
el garaje
garage

(soh-tah-noh)
el sótano
basement

While learning these new **palabras,** let's not forget:

(ow-toh-moh-veel)   *(koh-cheh)*
el automóvil / el coche
automobile, car

(moh-toh-see-kleh-tah)
la motocicleta
motorcycle

(bee-see-kleh-tah)
la bicicleta
bicycle

_____   _____   _____

❑	**el balcón** *(bahl-kohn)*	balcony	
❑	**la batalla** *(bah-tah-yah)*	battle	
❑	**el biftec** *(beef-tek)*....................	beefsteak	**b**
❑	**blando** *(blahn-doh)*	bland	
❑	**la botella** *(boh-teh-yah)*....................	bottle	

(gah-toh)
el gato
cat

(har-deen)
el jardín
garden

(floh-res)
las flores
flowers

el jardín, el jardín

_____

_____

_____

(peh-rroh)
el perro
dog

(boo-sohn)
el buzón
mailbox

(koh-rreh-oh)
el correo
mail

_____

_____

_____

Peel off the next set of labels **y** wander through your **casa** learning these new **palabras.** It will

be somewhat difficult to label **el gato,** *(gah-toh)* cat **las flores** *(floh-res)* flowers **o** *(oh)* or **el perro,** *(peh-rroh)* dog but be creative. Practice by

asking yourself, **"¿Dónde está el automóvil?"** *(ow-toh-moh-veel)* car and reply, **"Allí** *(ah-yee)* there **está el automóvil."**

¿Dónde está la casa?

❏ **el cálculo** *(kahl-koo-loh)*	calculation	
❏ **la calma** *(kahl-mah)*	calm	
❏ **la capital** *(kah-pee-tahl)*	capital	**c**
❏ **el carácter** *(kah-rahk-tair)*	character	
❏ **la causa** *(kow-sah)*	cause	

(oon-oh) *(dohs)* *(trehs)*
¡Uno, dos, tres!
one two three

Consider for a minute how important numbers are. How could you tell someone your phone

(oh)
number, your address **o** your hotel room if you had no numbers? And think of how difficult
or

(oh)
it would be if you could not understand the time, the price of an apple **o** the correct bus to

(noo-meh-rohs)
take. When practicing **los números** below, notice the similarities which have been underlined
numbers

(oh-choh) *(dee-eh-see-oh-choh)* *(see-eh-teh)* *(dee-eh-see-see-eh-teh)*
for you between **ocho** and **dieciocho,** **siete** and **diecisiete,** and so on.
eight eighteen seven seventeen

(seh-roh)		
0 cero		
(oon-oh)		
1 uno		
(dohs)		
2 dos		
(trehs)		
3 tres		
(kwah-troh)		
4 cuatro		
(seen-koh)		
5 cinco		
(sehs)		
6 seis		
(see-eh-teh)		
7 siete	*siete, siete, siete*	
(oh-choh)		
8 ocho		
(nweh-veh)		
9 nueve		
(dee-es)		
10 diez		

(dee-es)		
10 diez		
(ohn-seh)		
11 once		
(doh-seh)		
12 doce		
(treh-seh)		
13 trece		
(kah-tor-seh)		
14 catorce		
(keen-seh)		
15 quince		
(dee-eh-see-sehs)		
16 dieciséis		
(dee-eh-see-see-eh-teh)		
17 diecisiete		
(dee-eh-see-oh-choh)		
18 dieciocho		
(dee-eh-see-nweh-veh)		
19 diecinueve		
(vain-teh)		
20 veinte		

☑ **el centro** *(sen-troh)* . . . . center   *el centro, el centro, el centro*
☐ **el cheque** *(cheh-keh)* . . . . check
☐ **el chocolate** *(choh-koh-lah-teh)* . . . . chocolate   **c**
☐ **el círculo** *(seer-koo-loh)* . . . . circle
☐ **la civilización** *(see-vee-lee-sah-see-ohn)* . . . . . . civilization

Use these **números** *(noo-meh-rohs)* on a daily basis. Count to yourself **en español** *(es-pahn-yohl)* when you brush your teeth,

exercise **o** commute to work. Fill in the blanks below according to **los números** *(noo-meh-rohs)* given in

parentheses. Now is also a good time to learn these two very important phrases.

(yoh) (kee-yeh-roh)
yo quiero _____
I   want

(noh-soh-trohs)(keh-reh-mohs)
nosotros queremos _____
we   want

(yoh) (kee-yeh-roh)
Yo quiero _____ (1)
I   want

Yo quiero _____ (7)

Yo quiero _____ *ocho* (8)

Yo quiero _____ (5)

(noh-soh-trohs)(keh-reh-mohs)
Nosotros queremos _____ (9)
we   want

Nosotros queremos _____ (10)
we

Yo quiero _____ (1)

Nosotros queremos _____ (4)

Nosotros queremos _____ (11)

Yo quiero _____ (3)

Nosotros queremos _____ (4)

(tar-heh-tah) (pohs-tahl)
tarjeta postal.
postcard

(say-yohs)
sellos.
stamps

(say-yohs)
sellos.
stamps

(say-yohs)
sellos.
stamps

(tar-heh-tahs) (pohs-tah-les)
tarjetas postales.
postcards

(tar-heh-tahs)
tarjetas postales.

(bee-yeh-teh)
billete.
ticket

(bee-yeh-tes)
billetes.
tickets

(bee-yeh-tes)
billetes.

(tah-sahs) (teh)
tazas de té.
cups   of   tea

(vah-sohs)   (ah-gwah)
vasos de agua.
glasses   of   water

(kwahn-tahs)
¿Cuántas? _____ (1)
how many

¿Cuántos? _____ (7)

¿Cuántos? _____ (8)

¿Cuántos? _____ *cinco* (5)

¿Cuántas? _____ (9)

¿Cuántas? _____ (10)

¿Cuántos? _____ (1)

¿Cuántos? _____ (4)

¿Cuántos? _____ (11)

¿Cuántas? _____ (3)

(how many) _____ (4)

☐ **la clase** *(klah-seh)* . . . . class _____
☐ **la colección** *(koh-lek-see-ohn)* . . . . collection _____
☐ **cómico** *(koh-mee-koh)* . . . . comical **c** _____
☐ **la compañía** *(kohm-pahn-yee-ah)* . . . . company _____
☐ **la comunicación** *(koh-moo-nee-kah-see-ohn)* . . . . . communication _____

13

Now see if you can translate the following thoughts into **español**. The answers are provided

Spanish

upside down at the bottom of the **página**.

(pah-hee-nah)

page

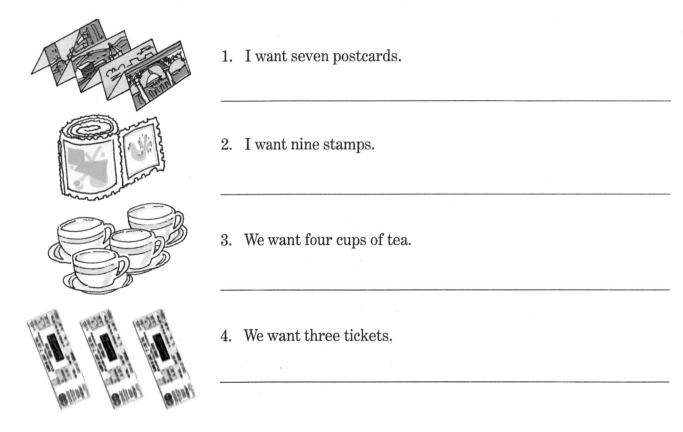

1. I want seven postcards.

_____

2. I want nine stamps.

_____

3. We want four cups of tea.

_____

4. We want three tickets.

_____

Review **los números** 1 through 20. Write out your telephone number, fax number, y cellular

number. Then write out a friend's telephone number and a relative's telephone number.

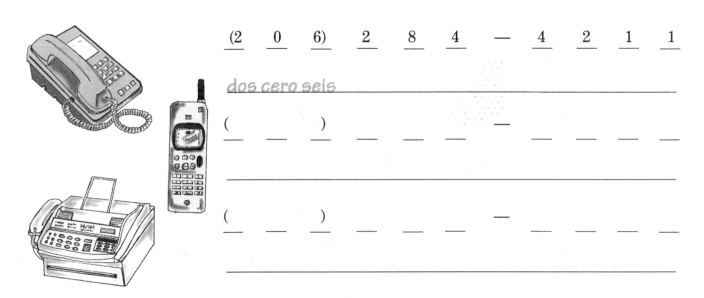

<u>(2</u> <u>0</u> <u>6)</u>   <u>2</u>   <u>8</u>   <u>4</u>   —   <u>4</u>   <u>2</u>   <u>1</u>   <u>1</u>

dos cero seis _____

(   )   —

_____

(   )   —

_____

6 (koh-loh-res) **Los Colores**
colors

Los colores son the same **en México** as they are **en los Estados Unidos** — they just have
(koh-loh-res)(sohn) · colors · are · *(es-tah-dohs)(oo-nee-dohs)* · in · United States

different **nombres**. You can easily recognize **violeta** as violet and **púrpura** as purple. So when
(nohm-bres) · names · *(vee-oh-leh-tah)* · *(poor-poo-rah)*

you are invited to someone's **casa y** you want to bring flowers, you will be able to order the color
(kah-sah) · house

you want. Let's learn the basic **colores**. Once you've learned **los colores,** quiz yourself. What
(koh-loh-res)

color are your shoes? Your eyes? Your hair? Your house?

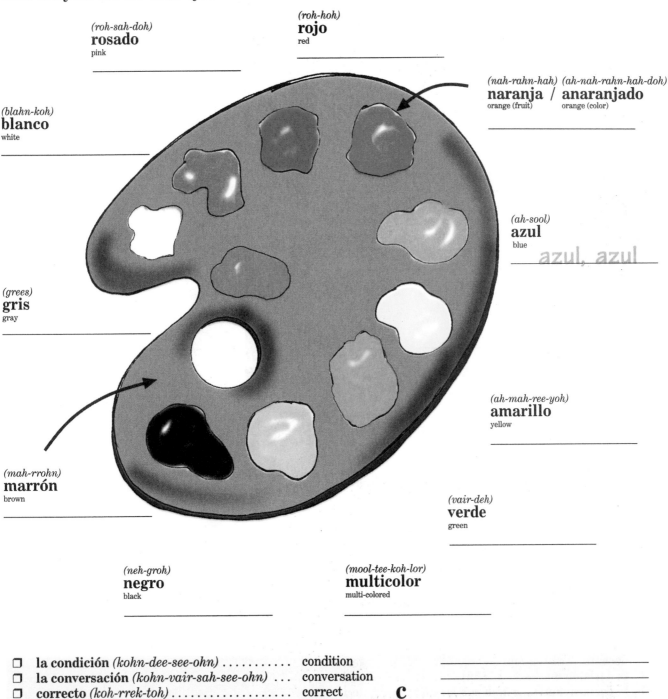

(roh-sah-doh)
rosado
pink
_____

(roh-hoh)
rojo
red
_____

(nah-rahn-hah) *(ah-nah-rahn-hah-doh)*
naranja / anaranjado
orange (fruit) · orange (color)
_____

(blahn-koh)
blanco
white
_____

(ah-sool)
azul
blue
azul, azul

(grees)
gris
gray
_____

(ah-mah-ree-yoh)
amarillo
yellow
_____

(mah-rrohn)
marrón
brown
_____

(vair-deh)
verde
green
_____

(neh-groh)
negro
black
_____

(mool-tee-koh-lor)
multicolor
multi-colored
_____

☐ **la condición** (*kohn-dee-see-ohn*) . . . . condition
☐ **la conversación** (*kohn-vair-sah-see-ohn*) . . . conversation
☐ **correcto** (*koh-rrek-toh*) . . . . correct **c**
☐ **la crema** (*kreh-mah*) . . . . cream
☐ **la cultura** (*kool-too-rah*) . . . . culture

_____
_____
_____
_____
_____

Peel off the next group of labels **y** (ee) proceed to label these **colores** in your **casa.** (kah-sah) house Identify the two **o** three dominant colors in the flags below.

Argentina _____

Bolivia _____

Chile _____

Colombia _____

Costa Rica _____

Ecuador _____

El Salvador _____

Guatemala _____

Honduras _____

México _____

Nicaragua _____

Panamá _____

Paraguay _____

Perú _____

Uruguay _____

Venezuela _____

In addition to Spain, you should be able to use your **español** (es-pahn-yohl) language skills in any of the above countries.

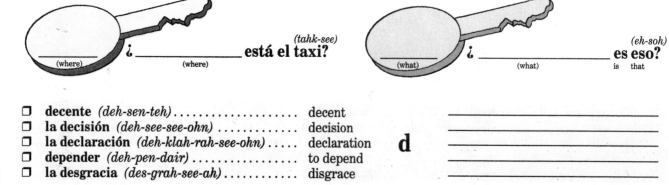

¿ _____ **está el taxi?** (tahk-see)
(where) (where)

¿ _____ **es eso?** (eh-soh)
(what) (what) is that

❒ **decente** (deh-sen-teh) . . . . decent
❒ **la decisión** (deh-see-see-ohn) . . . . decision
❒ **la declaración** (deh-klah-rah-see-ohn) . . . . . declaration
❒ **depender** (deh-pen-dair) . . . . to depend
❒ **la desgracia** (des-grah-see-ah) . . . . disgrace

d _____
_____
_____
_____

16

(lahm-pah-rah) la **lámpara**	*(ow-toh-moh-veel)* el **automóvil**	*(mah-rrohn)* **marrón**	*(sair-veh-sah)* la **cerveza**
(soh-fah) el **sofá**	*(moh-toh-see-kleh-tah)* la **motocicleta**	*(roh-hoh)* **rojo**	*(leh-cheh)* la **leche**
(see-yah) la **silla**	*(bee-see-kleh-tah)* la **bicicleta**	*(roh-sah-doh)* **rosado**	*(mahn-teh-kee-yah)* la **mantequilla**
(ahl-fohm-brah) la **alfombra**	*(gah-toh)* el **gato**	*(nah-rahn-hah)* **naranja**	*(sahl)* la **sal**
(meh-sah) la **mesa**	*(har-deen)* el **jardín**	*(blahn-koh)* **blanco**	*(pee-mee-en-tah)* la **pimienta**
(pwair-tah) la **puerta**	*(floh-res)* las **flores**	*(ah-mah-ree-yoh)* **amarillo**	*(vah-soh) (pah-rah) (vee-noh)* el **vaso para vino**
(reh-loh) el **reloj**	*(peh-rroh)* el **perro**	*(grees)* **gris**	*(vah-soh)* el **vaso**
(kor-tee-nah) la **cortina**	*(boo-sohn)* el **buzón**	*(neh-groh)* **negro**	*(peh-ree-oh-dee-koh)* el **periódico**
(teh-leh-foh-noh) el **teléfono**	*(koh-rreh-oh)* el **correo**	*(ah-sool)* **azul**	*(tah-sah)* la **taza**
(ven-tah-nah) la **ventana**	*(seh-roh)* 0 **cero**	*(vair-deh)* **verde**	*(teh-neh-dor)* el **tenedor**
(peen-too-rah) la **pintura**	*(oon-oh)* 1 **uno**	*(mool-tee-koh-lor)* **multicolor**	*(koo-chee-yoh)* el **cuchillo**
(kah-sah) la **casa**	*(dohs)* 2 **dos**	*(bweh-nohs) (dee-ahs)* **buenos días**	*(sair-vee-yeh-tah)* la **servilleta**
(oh-fee-see-nah) la **oficina**	*(trehs)* 3 **tres**	*(bweh-nahs) (tar-des)* **buenas tardes**	*(plah-toh)* el **plato**
(bahn-yoh) el **baño**	*(kwah-troh)* 4 **cuatro**	*(bweh-nahs) (noh-ches)* **buenas noches**	*(koo-chah-rah)* la **cuchara**
(koh-see-nah) la **cocina**	*(seen-koh)* 5 **cinco**	*(oh-lah)* **hola**	*(ar-mah-ree-oh)* el **armario**
(dor-mee-toh-ree-oh) el **dormitorio**	*(sehs)* 6 **seis**	*(ah-dee-ohs)* **adiós**	*(teh)* el **té**
(koh-meh-dor) el **comedor**	*(see-eh-teh)* 7 **siete**	*(koh-moh) (es-tah)* **¿Cómo está?**	*(kah-feh)* el **café**
(sah-lah) la **sala**	*(oh-choh)* 8 **ocho**	*(reh-free-heh-rah-dor)* el **refrigerador**	*(pahn)* el **pan**
(gah-rah-heh) el **garaje**	*(nweh-veh)* 9 **nueve**	*(or-noh)* el **horno**	*(por) (fah-vor)* **por favor**
(soh-tah-noh) el **sótano**	*(dee-es)* 10 **diez**	*(vee-noh)* el **vino**	*(grah-see-ahs)* **gracias**

STICKY LABELS

This book has over 150 special sticky labels for you to use as you learn new words. When you are introduced to one of these words, remove the corresponding label from these pages. Be sure to use each of these unique self-adhesive labels by adhering them to a picture, window, lamp, or whatever object it refers to. And yes, they are removable! The sticky labels make learning to speak Spanish much more fun and a lot easier than you ever expected. For example, when you look in the mirror and see the label, say

(es-peh-hoh)
"el espejo."
mirror

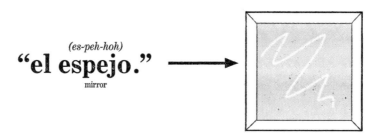

Don't just say it once, say it again and again. And once you label the refrigerator, you should never again open that door without saying

(reh-free-heh-rah-dor)
"el refrigerador."
refrigerator

By using the sticky labels, you not only learn new words, but friends and family learn along with you! The sooner you start, the sooner you can use these labels at home or work.

(dee-neh-roh)
El Dinero
money

Before starting this Step, go back and review Step 5. It is important that you can count to

(vain-teh) *(lee-broh)* *(noo-meh-rohs)*
veinte without looking at **el libro.** Let's learn the larger **números** now. After practicing aloud
twenty   book

(noo-meh-rohs)
los números en español 10 through 11,000 below, write these **números** in the blanks provided.

(sehs) *(dee-eh-see-sehs)*
Again, notice the similarities (underlined) between **números** such as <u>**seis**</u> (6), **dieci<u>séis</u>** (16),

(seh-sen-tah) *(sehs)* *(meel)*
<u>**se**</u>**senta** (60), **y** <u>**seis**</u> **mil** (6000).

10	*(dee-es)* **diez** _____	1.000	*(meel)* **mil** _____
20	*(vain-teh)* **veinte** _____	2.000	*(dohs) (meel)* **dos mil** _____
30	*(train-tah)* **treinta** _____	3.000	**tres mil** _____
40	*(kwah-ren-tah)* **cuarenta** *cuarenta, cuarenta*	4.000	**cuatro mil** _____
50	*(seen-kwen-tah)* **cincuenta** _____	5.000	**cinco mil** _____
60	*(seh-sen-tah)* **sesenta** _____	6.000	**seis mil** _____
70	*(seh-ten-tah)* <u>**setenta**</u> _____	7.000	**siete mil** _____
80	*(oh-chen-tah)* **ochenta** _____	8.000	**ocho mil** _____
90	*(noh-ven-tah)* **noventa** _____	9.000	**nueve mil** _____
100	*(see-en) (see-en-toh)* **cien/ ciento** _____	10.000	**diez mil** _____
500	*(kee-nee-en-tohs)* **quinientos** _____	10.500	*(dee-es) (kee-nee-en-tohs)* **diez mil quinientos** _____
1.000	*(meel)* **mil** _____	11.000	*(ohn-seh)* **once mil** _____

(ah-kee) *(dohs)*
Aquí are **dos** important phrases to go with all these **números.** Say them out loud over and over
here

and then write them out twice as many times.

(yoh) (tehn-goh)
yo tengo _____
I   have

(noh-soh-trohs) (teh-neh-mohs)
nosotros tenemos _____
we   have

Many English words that start with **sp** or **st** have an **e** in front of them in **español.**
- ❏ **espléndido** *(es-plen-dee-doh)* . . . . splendid   _____
- ❏ **la estación** *(es-tah-see-ohn)* . . . . station   _____
- ❏ **el estado** *(es-tah-doh)* . . . . state   **e**   _____
- ❏ **el estudiante** *(es-too-dee-ahn-teh)* . . . . student   _____

The unit of currency **en México** *(meh-hee-koh)* **es el peso,** *(peh-soh)* abbreviated "**$**" just like the American dollar. Let's

learn the various kinds of **monedas** *(moh-neh-dahs)* **y** *(ee)* **billetes.** *(bee-yeh-tes)* Always be sure to practice each **palabra** *(pah-lah-brah)* out
coins   bills

loud. You might want to exchange some money **ahora** *(ah-oh-rah)* so that you can familiarize yourself
now

con *(kohn)* the **varios** *(vah-ree-ohs)* **billetes y monedas.** *(bee-yeh-tes)* *(moh-neh-dahs)*
with   various

en México *(meh-hee-koh)*

veinte pesos *(vain-teh)*

cincuenta pesos *(seen-kwen-tah)*

cien pesos *(see-en)*

en España *(es-pahn-yah)*

diez euros *(dee-es)*

cincuenta euros *(seen-kwen-tah)*

en Argentina *(ar-hen-tee-nah)*

dos pesos

cinco pesos

en Costa Rica *(koh-stah)* *(ree-kah)*

mil colones *(koh-loh-nes)*

cinco mil colones

❏ **la diferencia** *(dee-feh-ren-see-ah)*	difference	
❏ **la distancia** *(dees-tan-see-ah)*	distance	
❏ **la división** *(dee-vee-see-ohn)*	division	**d**
❏ **el doctor** *(dohk-tor)*	doctor	
❏ **el documento** *(doh-koo-men-toh)*	document	

Review **los números** *(noo-meh-rohs)* **diez** through **mil** *(meel)* again. **Ahora,** **cómo** do you say "twenty-two" **o** *(oh)*
now   how

"fifty-three" **en español?** Put the numbers together in a logical sequence just as you do in

English. See if you can say **y** *(ee)* write out **los números** *(noo-meh-rohs)* on this **página.** *(pah-hee-nah)* The answers **están** *(es-tahn)* at
page   are

the bottom of the **página.** *(pah-hee-nah)*

1. _____   2. _____
(25 = 20 + 5)   (83 = 80 + 3)

3. _____   4. __noventa y seis__
(47 = 40 + 7)   (96 = 90 + 6)

Now, **cómo** *(koh-moh)* would you say the following **en español?** *(es-pahn-yohl)*

5. _____
(I have 80 pesos.)

6. _____
(We have 72 pesos.)

To ask how much something costs **en español,** *(es-pahn-yohl)* one asks — **¿Cuánto cuesta esto?** *(kwahn-toh) (kwes-tah) (es-toh)*

Now you try it. _____
(How much does that cost?)

Answer the following questions based on the numbers in parentheses.

7. **¿Cuánto cuesta esto? Cuesta** *(kwahn-toh)* _____ **pesos.**
   costs this   (10)

8. **¿Cuánto cuesta esto? Cuesta** *(kwes-tah)* _____ **pesos.**
   (20)

9. **¿Cuánto cuesta el libro? El libro cuesta** *(lee-broh)* _____ **pesos.**
   book   (17)

10. **¿Cuánto cuesta la tarjeta postal? La tarjeta postal cuesta** *(tar-heh-tah) (pohs-tahl)* _____ **pesos.**
    postcard   (2)

ANSWERS

1. veinte y cinco	6. Nosotros tenemos setenta y dos pesos.
2. ochenta y tres	7. diez
3. cuarenta y siete	8. veinte
4. noventa y seis	9. diecisiete
5. Yo tengo ochenta pesos.	10. dos

(kah-len-dah-ree-oh)
El calendario
calendar

———————————

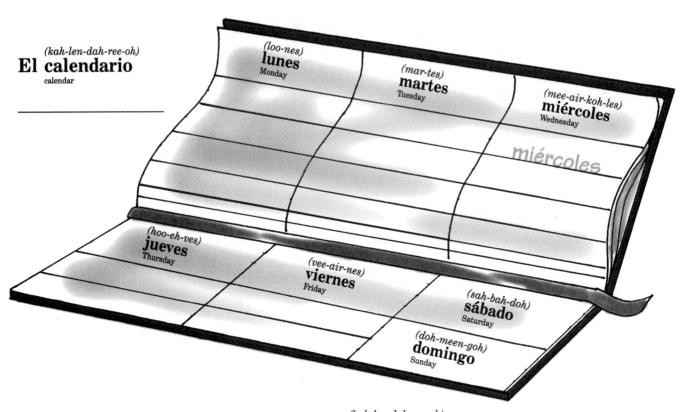

(loo-nes) **lunes** Monday

(mar-tes) **martes** Tuesday

(mee-air-koh-les) **miércoles** Wednesday

miércoles

(hoo-eh-ves) **jueves** Thursday

(vee-air-nes) **viernes** Friday

(sah-bah-doh) **sábado** Saturday

(doh-meen-goh) **domingo** Sunday

Learn the days of the week by writing them in **el calendario** *(kah-len-dah-ree-oh)* above **y** then move on to the

(kwah-troh) **cuatro** parts to each *(dee-ah)* **día.**
four   day

(mahn-yah-nah)
la mañana
morning

(tar-deh)
la tarde
afternoon

(noh-cheh)
la noche
evening

(noh-cheh)
la noche
night

———————————   ———————————   ———————————   ———————————

☐ **la economía** *(eh-koh-noh-mee-ah)* .... economy _____
☐ **eléctrico** *(eh-lek-tree-koh)* .... electric _____
☐ **enorme** *(eh-nor-meh)* .... enormous   **e** _____
☐ **entrar** *(en-trar)* .... to enter _____
☐ **el error** *(eh-rror)* .... error _____

It is **muy** *(mwee)* **importante** *(eem-por-tahn-teh)* to know the days of the week **y** the various parts of the day as well as

^{very} ^{important}

these **tres palabras.**

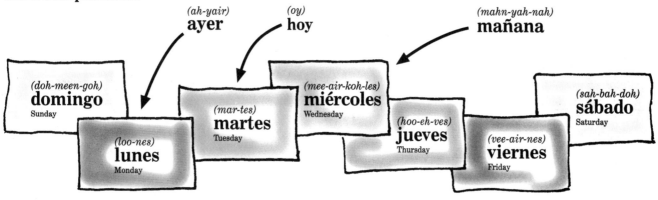

(ah-yair) **ayer**　　*(oy)* **hoy**　　*(mahn-yah-nah)* **mañana**

(doh-meen-goh) **domingo** Sunday

(loo-nes) **lunes** Monday

(mar-tes) **martes** Tuesday

(mee-air-koh-les) **miércoles** Wednesday

(hoo-eh-ves) **jueves** Thursday

(vee-air-nes) **viernes** Friday

(sah-bah-doh) **sábado** Saturday

¿Qué día *(dee-ah)* **es hoy?** _____ 　**¿Qué día es mañana?** *(mahn-yah-nah)* _____

^{what}

¿Qué día fue ayer? *(fweh) (ah-yair)* _____ 　**¿Hoy es martes, sí?** So, _____

^{was} 　　　　　　　　　　　　　　　　　　　　　　　　　　　^{yes}　　　　_(tomorrow)

es miércoles y _____ **fue** *(fweh)* **lunes.** Remember "**mañana**" means both "morning" **y**

_(yesterday)　　　^{was}

"tomorrow" **en español.** Notice that "**por**" comes after the day of the week in the exercise below.

ⁱⁿ

a.　on Sunday morning　　=　_____

b.　on Friday morning　　=　_____

c.　on Saturday evening　　=　_____

d.　on Thursday afternoon　=　_____ jueves por la tarde _____

e.　on Thursday night　　=　_____

f.　yesterday evening　　=　_____

g.　tomorrow afternoon　　=　_____

h.　tomorrow evening　　=　_____

_____ ¿ _____ **es el concierto?** *(kohn-see-air-toh)*
_(when)　_(when)　　　　　　^{concert}

_____ ¿ _____ **es?**
_(who)　_(who)　　^{is it}

ANSWERS

		c. sábado por la noche
	f. ayer por la noche	
h. mañana por la noche	e. jueves por la noche	b. viernes por la mañana
g. mañana por la tarde	d. jueves por la tarde	a. domingo por la mañana

Knowing the parts of **el día** *(dee-ah)* / day will help you to learn the various **español** greetings below.

Practice these every day until your trip.

(bweh-nohs)(dee-ahs)
buenos días _____
good morning/good day

(bweh-nahs)(tar-des)
buenas tardes _____
good   afternoon

(bweh-nahs)(noh-ches)
buenas noches _____
good evening/good night

(oh-lah)
hola _____
hello/hi

Take the next **cuatro** *(kwah-troh)* / four labels **y** stick them on the appropriate things in your **casa** *(kah-sah)* / house. Make sure

you attach them to the correct items, as they are only **en español.** How about the bathroom

mirror for "**buenos días**" *(bweh-nohs)*? **o** *(oh)* / or your alarm clock for "**buenas noches**"? Let's not forget,

(koh-moh) (es-tah)
¿Cómo está? _____
how are you

Now for some " **sí** *(see)* / yes " or " **no** *(no)* / no " questions –

Are your eyes **azul** *(ah-sool)*? _____   Are your shoes **marrón** *(mah-rrohn)*? _____

Is your favorite color **rojo** *(roh-hoh)*? _____   Is today **sábado** *(sah-bah-doh)*? _____

Do you own a **perro** *(peh-rroh)*? _____   Do you own a **gato** *(gah-toh)*? _____

You are about one-fourth of your way through this **libro** *(lee-broh)* / book **y** it is a good time to quickly review

las palabras you have learned before doing the crossword puzzle on the next **página** *(pah-hee-nah)*. Have

fun **y buena suerte!** *(bweh-nah)(swair-teh)*
good   luck

ANSWERS TO THE CROSSWORD PUZZLE

ACROSS

4. día	25. hoy	39. lunes	52. billete
5. bicicleta	28. sábado	41. correo	51. trece
11. ayer	34. decente	44. casa	50. familia
13. alfombra	34. cuesta		47. nosotros
14. activo	36. ¿por qué?		46. noche
16. marrón	38. sí		54. mesa
17. sala	39. lunes		56. sellos
19. doctor			
23. abril			

DOWN

1. mañana	18. peso	35. silla	
2. calma	19. diez	37. quién	
3. uno	21. rosado	40. eso	
6. civilización	22. cocina	42. teléfono	
7. estado	26. balcón	45. seis	
8. carácter	30. tres	48. treinta	
9. tengo	31. perro	49. causa	
10. lámpara	32. de	53. exacto	
12. yo	33. cero	55. inglés	

CROSSWORD PUZZLE

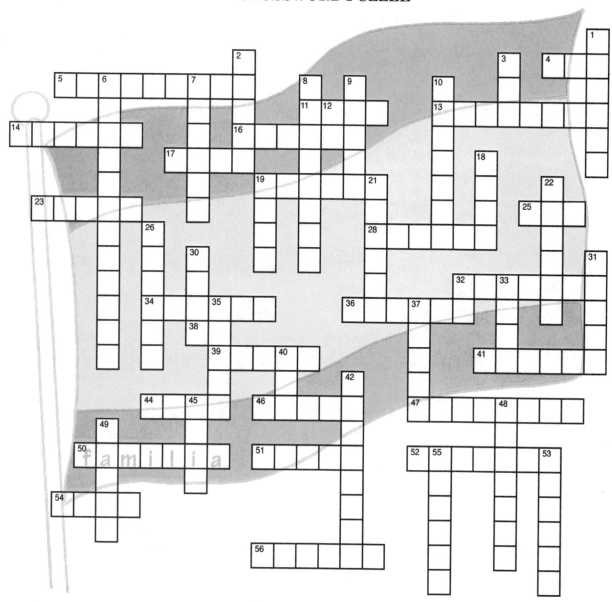

ACROSS

4. day
5. bicycle
11. yesterday
13. carpet
14. active
16. brown
17. living room
19. doctor
23. April
25. today
28. Saturday
32. decent
34. (it) costs
36. why
38. yes
39. Monday
41. mail
44. house
46. night
47. we
50. family
51. thirteen
52. bill, ticket
54. table
56. stamps

DOWN

1. morning, tomorrow
2. calm
3. one
6. civilization
7. state
8. character
9. (I) have
10. lamp
12. I
18. Mexican currency
19. ten
21. pink
22. kitchen
26. balcony
30. three
31. dog
32. of
33. zero
35. chair
37. who
40. that
42. telephone
45. six
48. thirty
49. cause
53. exact
55. English

❏ **exacto** *(ek-sahk-toh)* . . . . exact
❏ **excelente** *(ek-seh-len-teh)* . . . . excellent
❏ **existir** *(ek-sees-teer)* . . . . to exist   **e**
❏ **la expresión** *(es-preh-see-ohn)* . . . . expression
❏ **el extremo** *(es-treh-moh)* . . . . extreme

(en) *(deh)* *(soh-breh)*
En, de, sobre...
in   from   on top of

(es-pahn-yohl)
Español prepositions (words like "in," "on," "through" and "next to") **son** easy to learn, **y**
Spanish   *(sohn)* are

they allow you to be **preciso** **con** a **mínimo** of effort. Instead of having to point **cuatro** times
(preh-see-soh) precise   *(mee-nee-moh)* minimum

at a piece of yummy pastry you would like, you can explain precisely which one you want by

saying **está** behind, in front of, next to **o** under the piece of pastry that the salesperson is
it is   *(oh)*

starting to pick up. Let's learn some of these little **palabras.**

(deh-bah-hoh)
debajo de _____
under/below

(en)
en _____
into/in/on

(soh-breh)
sobre _____
over/on top of/above

(deh-lahn-teh)
delante de _____
in front of

(en-treh)
entre ____ entre, entre, entre ____
between

(deh-trahs)
detrás de _____
behind

(ahl) (lah-doh) (deh)
al lado de _____
next to

(deh)
de _____
of/from

(ah)
a _____
to/at

(pahs-tel)
pastel _____
cake, pie, pastry!

Note that "**a**" and "**de**" combine with "**el**" to form "**al**" and "**del**." Fill in the blanks on the next
(a+el) *(de+el)*

(pah-hee-nah)
página with the correct prepositions.

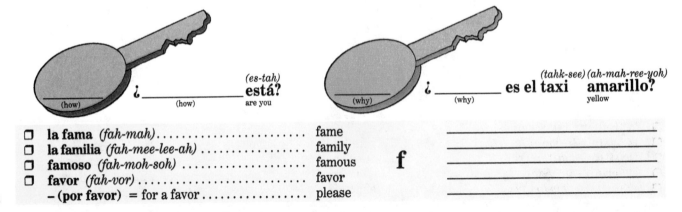

(es-tah)
¿_____ **está?**
(how) (how) are you

(tahk-see) (ah-mah-ree-yoh)
¿_____ es el taxi amarillo?
(why) (why)   yellow

☐	**la fama** *(fah-mah)*	fame
☐	**la familia** *(fah-mee-lee-ah)*	family
☐	**famoso** *(fah-moh-soh)*	famous
☐	**favor** *(fah-vor)*	favor
	– (**por favor**) = for a favor	please

f

_____
_____
_____
_____

El *(pahs-tel)* **pastel está** _____ **la** *(meh-sah)* **mesa.**
pastry   (on)   table

El *(peh-rroh)* **perro negro está** _____ **la mesa.**
dog   (under)   table

El *(dohk-tor)* **doctor está** _____ **el hotel** *(nweh-voh)* **nuevo.**
doctor   (in)

¿Dónde está el doctor? _____

El *(ohm-breh)* **hombre está** _____ **hotel.**
man   (in front of)

¿Dónde está el hombre? _____

El *(teh-leh-foh-noh)* **teléfono está** _____ **la** *(peen-too-rah)* **pintura.**
telephone   (next to)   picture

¿Dónde está el teléfono? _____

(ah-or-ah)
Ahora fill in each blank on the picture below with the best possible one of these *(peh-kehn-yahs)* **pequeñas**
now   little

palabras. Will you be attending **una** *(koh-rree-dah)* **corrida** *(toh-rohs)* **de toros** while abroad?
       bullfight

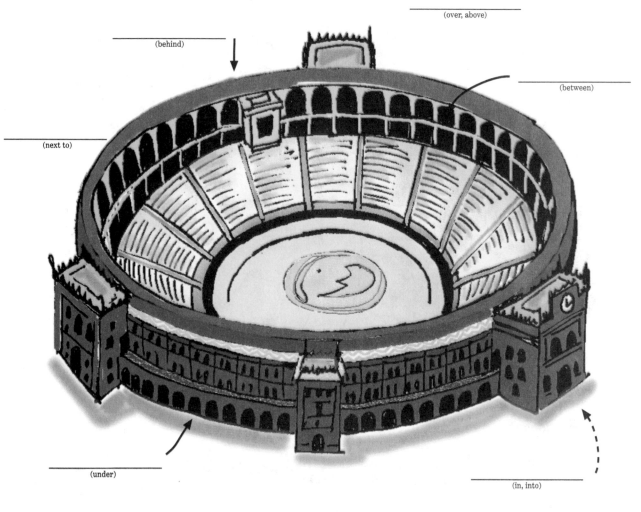

_____ (over, above)

_____ (behind)

_____ (between)

_____ (next to)

_____ (under)

_____ (in, into)

_____ (in front of)

☐ **la ficción** *(feek-see-ohn)* . . . . fiction
☐ **la figura** *(fee-goo-rah)* . . . . figure
☐ **final** *(fee-nahl)* . . . . final
☐ **la forma** *(for-mah)* . . . . form
☐ **la fortuna** *(for-too-nah)* . . . . fortune

f

_____
_____
_____
_____
_____

(eh-neh-roh) *(feh-breh-roh)* *(mar-soh)*
Enero, Febrero, Marzo
January   February   March

(seh-mah-nah)   *(oh-rah)*   *(meh-ses)* *(ahn-yoh)*

You have learned **los días de la semana,** so now **es hora** to learn **los meses del año** y all the
days   of   week   it is   time   months   of the   year

(tee-em-poh)
different kinds of **tiempo.**
weather

(eh-neh-roh) **enero** 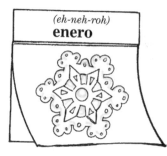	*(feh-breh-roh)* **febrero** 	*(mar-soh)* **marzo** 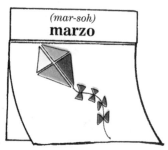	*(ah-breel)* **abril** 
(mah-yoh) **mayo** 	*(hoo-nee-oh)* **junio** 	*(hoo-lee-oh)* **julio** 	*(ah-gohs-toh)* **agosto** 
(sep-tee-em-breh) **septiembre** 	*(ohk-too-breh)* **octubre** 	*(noh-vee-em-breh)* **noviembre** 	*(dee-see-em-breh)* **diciembre** 

(keh) *(tee-em-poh)* *(ah-seh)* *(oy)*

When someone asks, "**¿Qué tiempo hace hoy?**" you have a variety of answers. Let's learn
what   is the weather   today

them but first, does this sound familiar?

(train-tah)   *(tee-en-eh)* *(sep-tee-em-breh)* *(ah-breel)* *(hoo-nee-oh)*   *(noh-vee-em-breh)*
Treinta días tiene septiembre, abril, junio y noviembre . . .
has

☐ **la foto** *(foh-toh)*	photograph	
☐ **frecuente** *(freh-kwen-teh)*	frequent	
☐ **la fruta** *(froo-tah)*	fruit	**f**
☐ **el fugitivo** *(foo-hee-tee-voh)*	fugitive	
☐ **el futuro** *(foo-too-roh)*	future	

(tee-em-poh)
¿Qué tiempo hace hoy? _____
what _____ today

(nee-eh-vah)
Nieva **en enero.** _____
it snows _____ in

(tahm-bee-en)
Nieva también en febrero. _____
also

(yweh-veh)
Llueve en marzo. _____
it rains

(tahm-bee-en)
Llueve también en abril. _____

(ah-ee) (vee-en-toh)
Hay viento en mayo. _____
there is _ wind

(hoo-nee-oh)
Hay viento también en junio. _____

(ah-seh) (kah-lor) (hoo-lee-oh)
Hace calor en julio. _____
it makes _ heat

(ah-gohs-toh)
Hace calor también en agosto. _____

(bwen) (tee-em-poh)
Hace buen tiempo en septiembre. _____

(ah-ee) (nee-eh-blah) (ohk-too-breh)
Hay niebla en octubre. _____
there is _ fog

(ah-seh) (free-oh)
Hace frío en noviembre. _____
cold

(mahl)
Hace mal tiempo en diciembre. _____
bad

(tee-em-poh)
¿Qué tiempo hace en febrero? _____

(ah-seh)
¿Qué tiempo hace en abril? _____ Llueve en abril. _____

(keh)
¿Qué tiempo hace en mayo? _____

¿Qué tiempo hace en agosto? _____

☐ **la gasolina** *(gah-soh-lee-nah)* . . . . gas _____
☐ **la gloria** *(gloh-ree-ah)* . . . . glory _____
☐ **grave** *(grah-veh)* . . . . grave, serious **g** _____
☐ **el grupo** *(groo-poh)* . . . . group _____
☐ **guardar** *(gwar-dar)* . . . . to guard, to keep _____

Ahora for the seasons **del año...**
(ahn-yoh)
of the year

(een-vee-air-noh)
el invierno
winter

(veh-rah-noh)
el verano
summer

(oh-tohn-yoh)
el otoño
autumn

(pree-mah-veh-rah)
la primavera
spring

(sen-tee-grah-doh)
Centígrado
Centigrade

(fah-ren-hite)
Fahrenheit
Fahrenheit

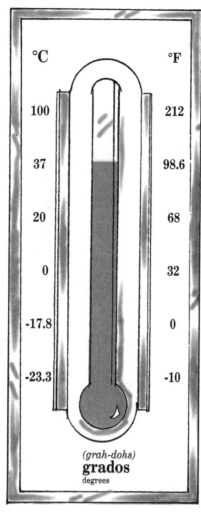

°C	°F
100	212
37	98.6
20	68
0	32
-17.8	0
-23.3	-10

(grah-dohs)
grados
degrees

At this point, **es una buena idea** to familiarize
(bweh-nah)(ee-deh-ah)
good
yourself **con las temperaturas.** Carefully study
(kohn) *(tem-peh-rah-too-rahs)*
temperatures
el termómetro because **las temperaturas en**
(tair-moh-meh-troh) *(tem-peh-rah-too-rahs)*

México y en España are calculated on the basis of

Centigrade (not Fahrenheit).

To convert °F to °C, subtract 32 and multiply by 0.55.

$$98.6\,°F - 32 = 66.6 \times 0.55 = 37\,°C$$

To convert °C to °F, multiply by 1.8 and add 32.

$$37\,°C \times 1.8 = 66.6 + 32 = 98.6\,°F$$

What is normal body temperature in **Centígrado?**

What is the freezing point in **Centígrado?**

☐ **habitual** *(ah-bee-too-ahl)* .... habitual _____
☐ **la historia** *(ees-toh-ree-ah)* .... history _____
☐ **honesto** *(oh-nes-toh)* .... honest, decent **h** _____
☐ **el honor** *(oh-nor)* .... honor _____
☐ **el humor** *(oo-mor)* .... humor _____

11

(mee) (kah-sah) (soo)
¡Mi casa es su casa!
my home your home

En México, not just the parents, but also the grandparents, aunts, uncles and cousins are all

considered as close **familia.** *(fah-mee-lee-ah)* family   Study the family tree below. Men carry the mother's maiden

name after the father's last name, although only the father's last name is used in addressing

the person.

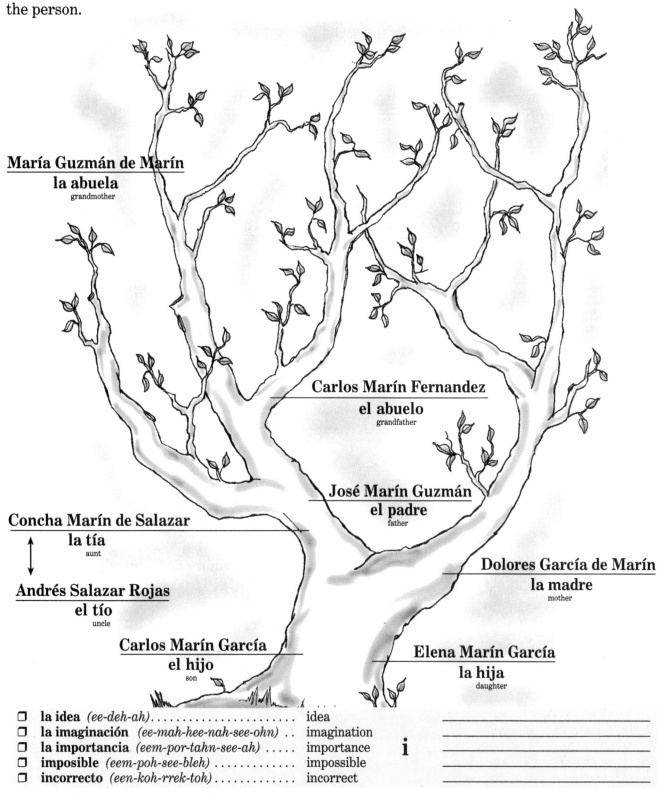

María Guzmán de Marín
la abuela
grandmother

Carlos Marín Fernandez
el abuelo
grandfather

José Marín Guzmán
el padre
father

Concha Marín de Salazar
la tía
aunt

Andrés Salazar Rojas
el tío
uncle

Dolores García de Marín
la madre
mother

Carlos Marín García
el hijo
son

Elena Marín García
la hija
daughter

❏ **la idea** *(ee-deh-ah)*...................... idea
❏ **la imaginación** *(ee-mah-hee-nah-see-ohn)* .. imagination
❏ **la importancia** *(eem-por-tahn-see-ah)* ..... importance
❏ **imposible** *(eem-poh-see-bleh)* .... impossible
❏ **incorrecto** *(een-koh-rrek-toh)* .... incorrect

i

_____
_____
_____
_____
_____

31

Let's learn how to identify **la familia** *(fah-mee-lee-ah)* by **nombre** *(nohm-breh)*. Study the following **ejemplos** *(eh-hem-plohs)* carefully.

family / name / examples

¿Cómo se llama? *(yah-mah)* _____
what is your name/how are you called

Me llamo *(yah-moh)* _____
my name is/I am called   (your name)

los padres *(pah-drehs)*
parents

el padre *(pah-dreh)* _____
father

¿Cuál es el nombre del padre? *(kwahl)* *(de+el)* _____
what   name   of the father

la madre *(mah-dreh)* _____
mother

¿Cuál es el nombre de la madre? *(kwahl)* _____
what   mother

los hijos *(ee-hohs)*   **el hijo y la hija** *(ee-hoh)* *(ee-hah)* = **hermano y hermana** *(air-mah-noh)* *(air-mah-nah)*
children   brother   sister

el hijo *(ee-hoh)* _____
son

¿Cuál es el nombre del hijo? *(ee-hoh)* _____
what   name   son

la hija *(ee-hah)* _____
daughter

¿Cuál es el nombre de la hija? *(ee-hah)* _____
daughter

los parientes *(pah-ree-en-tes)*
relatives

el abuelo *(ah-bweh-loh)* _____
grandfather

¿Cuál es el nombre del abuelo? *(ah-bweh-loh)* _____
grandfather

la abuela *(ah-bweh-lah)* _____
grandmother

¿Cuál es el nombre de la abuela? *(ah-bweh-lah)* _____
grandmother

Now you ask —

And answer —

_____
(How are you called?/What is your name?)

_____
(My name is . . .)

❏ **la influencia** *(een-floo-en-see-ah)* .... influence   _____
❏ **la información** *(een-for-mah-see-ohn)* .... information   _____
❏ **inglés** *(een-gles)*........................ English   **i**   _____
❏ **la instrucción** *(een-strook-see-ohn)* .... instruction   _____
❏ **el instrumento** *(een-stroo-men-toh)* .... instrument   _____

(koh-see-nah)
La Cocina
kitchen / stove

(reh-free-heh-rah-dor)
el refrigerador
refrigerator

(or-noh)
el horno
oven

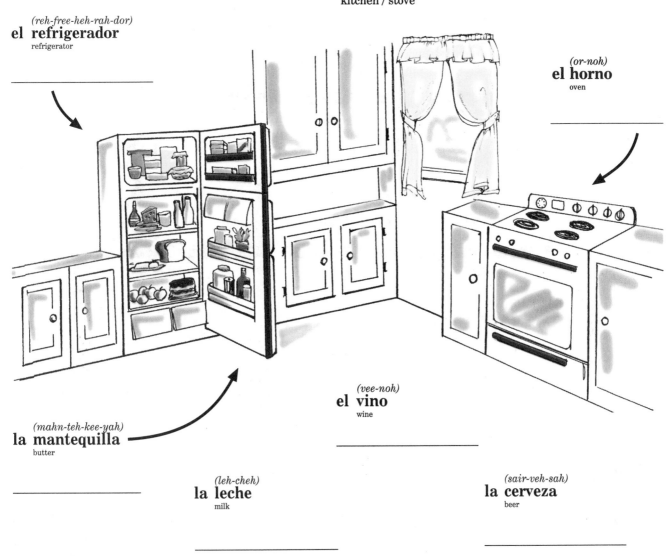

(mahn-teh-kee-yah)
la mantequilla
butter

(vee-noh)
el vino
wine

(leh-cheh)
la leche
milk

(sair-veh-sah)
la cerveza
beer

Answer these questions aloud.

(sair-veh-sah)
¿Dónde está la cerveza? . . . . *(reh-free-heh-rah-dor)* **La cerveza está en el refrigerador.**
beer

(leh-cheh)
¿Dónde está la leche?
milk

(vee-noh)
¿Dónde está el vino ?
wine

(mahn-teh-kee-yah)
¿Dónde está la mantequilla?
butter

(ah-brah) *(lee-broh)*
Ahora abra your **libro** to the **página con** the labels **y** remove the next group of labels **y**
open   book

(koh-sahs) *(koh-see-nah)*
proceed to label all these **cosas** in your **cocina.**
things   kitchen

☐	**la inteligencia** *(een-teh-lee-hen-see-ah)*	intelligence
☐	**la intención** *(een-ten-see-ohn)*	intention
☐	**interesante** *(een-teh-reh-sahn-teh)*	interesting **i**
☐	**el interior** *(een-teh-ree-or)*	interior
☐	**invitar** *(een-vee-tar)*	to invite

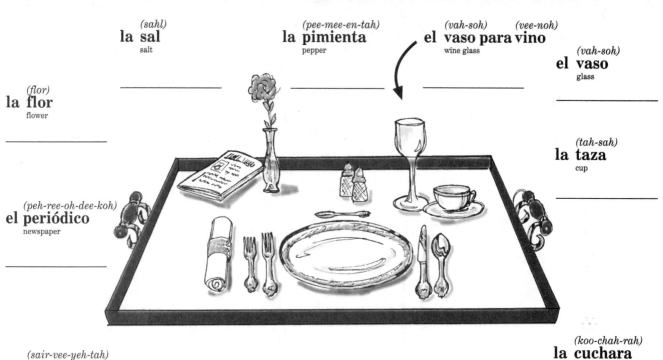

la sal *(sahl)*
salt

la pimienta *(pee-mee-en-tah)*
pepper

el vaso para vino *(vah-soh) (vee-noh)*
wine glass

el vaso *(vah-soh)*
glass

la flor *(flor)*
flower

_____

la taza *(tah-sah)*
cup

el periódico *(peh-ree-oh-dee-koh)*
newspaper

_____

la servilleta *(sair-vee-yeh-tah)*
napkin

_____

el tenedor *(teh-neh-dor)*
fork

el plato *(plah-toh)*
plate

el cuchillo *(koo-chee-yoh)*
knife

la cuchara *(koo-chah-rah)*
spoon

_____

_____ _____ _____

Y more . . .

el armario *(ar-mah-ree-oh)* _____
cupboard

el té *(teh)* _____ **¿Dónde está el té?** *(dohn-deh)*
tea

El té está en el armario. *(ar-mah-ree-oh)*

el café *(kah-feh)* _____ **¿Dónde está el café?**
coffee

el pan *(pahn)* _____ **¿Dónde está el pan?**
bread

Don't forget to label all these things and do not forget to use every

oportunidad *(oh-por-too-nee-dahd)* to say these **palabras** out loud. **Es muy importante.** *(mwee) (eem-por-tahn-teh)*
opportunity   very

☐	**julio** *(hoo-lee-oh)*	July		_____
☐	**junio** *(hoo-nee-oh)*	June	**j**	_____
☐	**la justicia** *(hoos-tee-see-ah)*	justice		_____
☐	**juvenil** *(hoo-veh-neel)*	juvenile		_____
☐	**el kilómetro** *(kee-loh-meh-troh)*	kilometer	**k**	_____

(pair-doh-neh-meh) **perdóneme**	*(say-yoh)* el **sello**	*(pay-neh)* el **peine**	*(pahn-tah-loh-nes)(kor-tohs)* los **pantalones cortos**
(kah-mah) la **cama**	*(tar-heh-tah)* *(pohs-tahl)* la **tarjeta postal**	*(ah-bree-goh)* el **abrigo**	*(kah-mee-seh-tah)* la **camiseta**
(ahl-moh-hah-dah) la **almohada**	*(pah-sah-por-teh)* el **pasaporte**	*(pah-rah-gwahs)* el **paraguas**	*(kahl-sohn-see-yohs)* los **calzoncillos**
(mahn-tah) la **manta**	*(bee-yeh-teh)* *(ah-vee-ohn)* el **billete de avión**	*(eem-pair-meh-ah-bleh)* el **impermeable**	*(kah-mee-seh-tah)* la **camiseta**
(des-pair-tah-dor) el **despertador**	*(mah-leh-tah)* la **maleta**	*(gwahn-tes)* los **guantes**	*(ves-tee-doh)* el **vestido**
(es-peh-hoh) el **espejo**	*(bohl-sah)* la **bolsa**	*(sohm-breh-roh)* el **sombrero**	*(bloo-sah)* la **blusa**
(lah-vah-boh) el **lavabo**	*(kar-teh-rah)* la **cartera**	*(sohm-breh-roh)* el **sombrero**	*(fahl-dah)* la **falda**
(toh-ah-yahs) las **toallas**	*(dee-neh-roh)* el **dinero**	*(boh-tahs)* las **botas**	*(sweh-tair)* el **suéter**
(es-koo-sah-doh) el **excusado**	*(tar-heh-tahs)* *(kreh-dee-toh)* las **tarjetas de crédito**	*(sah-pah-tohs)* los **zapatos**	*(kohm-bee-nah-see-ohn)* la **combinación**
(doo-chah) la **ducha**	*(cheh-kes)* *(vee-ah-heh-roh)* los **cheques de viajero**	*(sah-pah-tohs)* *(teh-nees)* los **zapatos de tenis**	*(sohs-ten)* el **sostén**
(lah-pees) el **lápiz**	*(kah-mah-rah)* la **cámara**	*(trah-heh)* el **traje**	*(kahl-sohn-see-yohs)* los **calzoncillos**
(teh-leh-vee-sor) el **televisor**	*(roh-yoh)* *(peh-lee-koo-lah)* el **rollo de película**	*(kor-bah-tah)* la **corbata**	*(kahl-seh-tee-nes)* los **calcetines**
(ploo-mah) la **pluma**	*(trah-heh)* *(bahn-yoh)* el **traje de baño**	*(kah-mee-sah)* la **camisa**	*(meh-dee-ahs)* las **medias**
(reh-vees-tah) la **revista**	*(sahn-dah-lee-ahs)* las **sandalias**	*(pahn-yweh-loh)* el **pañuelo**	*(pee-hah-mah)* el **pijama**
(lee-broh) el **libro**	*(gah-fahs)* *(sohl)* las **gafas de sol**	*(chah-keh-tah)* la **chaqueta**	*(kah-mee-sah)* *(dor-meer)* la **camisa de dormir**
(kohm-poo-tah-dor-ah) la **computadora**	*(seh-pee-yoh)* *(dee-en-tes)* el **cepillo de dientes**	*(pahn-tah-loh-nes)* los **pantalones**	*(bah-tah)* *(bahn-yoh)* la **bata de baño**
(gah-fahs) las **gafas**	*(pahs-tah)* *(dee-en-tes)* la **pasta de dientes**	*(vah-keh-rohs)* los **vaqueros**	*(sah-pah-tee-yahs)* las **zapatillas**
(pah-pel) el **papel**	*(hah-bohn)* el **jabón**	*(soy)* *(deh)* Yo **soy de** _____ .	
(ses-toh) *(pah-rah)* *(pah-peh-les)* el **cesto para papeles**	*(nah-vah-hah)* *(ah-fay-tar)* la **navaja de afeitar**	*(kee-air-oh)* *(ah-pren-dair)* *(es-pahn-yohl)* **Quiero aprender el español.**	
(kar-tah) la **carta**	*(des-oh-doh-rahn-teh)* el **desodorante**	*(mee)* *(nom-breh)* *(es)* Mi **nombre es** _____ .	

PLUS . . .

This book includes a number of other innovative features unique to the *"10 minutes a day®"* series. At the back of this book, you will find twelve pages of flash cards. Cut them out and flip through them at least once a day.

On pages 116, 117 and 118 you will find a beverage guide and a menu guide. Don't wait until your trip to use them. Clip out the menu guide and use it tonight at the dinner table. Take them both with you the next time you dine at your favorite Spanish or Mexican restaurant.

By using the special features in this book, you will be speaking Spanish before you know it.

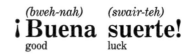

(bweh-nah) *(swair-teh)*
¡ Buena suerte!
good luck

(reh-lee-hee-ohn)
La Religión
religion

(meh-hee-koh)   *(vah-ree-eh-dahd)*   *(reh-lee-hee-oh-nes)*   *(noh-soh-trohs)*
En México there is not the wide **variedad** of **religiones** that **nosotros** find **en los**
                                              variety   religions

(es-tah-dohs) (oo-nee-dohs)   *(reh-lee-hee-ohn)*
Estados Unidos. A person's **religión** is usually one of the following.

(kah-toh-lee-koh)
1. **católico** _____
   Catholic

(proh-tes-tahn-teh)
2. **protestante** _____
   Protestant

(hoo-dee-oh)
3. **judío** _____
   Jewish

(ee-gleh-see-ah) (meh-hee-kah-nah)
Aquí está una iglesia mexicana.
                    church
                    (kah-toh-lee-kah)
¿Es una iglesia católica?
  is it

¿Es una iglesia protestante?

(nweh-vah)
¿Es una iglesia nueva?
                    new
                    (vee-eh-hah)
¿Es una iglesia vieja?
                    old

(ah-oh-rah)   *(es-pahn-yohl) (yoh) (soy)*
Ahora, let's learn how to say "I am" **en español: yo soy** _____
now   I   am

                                                   (es-toy)
                                              yo estoy _____
                                                I   am

                                                                                   (bee-en)
Use "**yo estoy**" when you are telling your location or how you feel, for example, "**Yo estoy bien,**" or
                                                                                        well
(bee-en)
simply, "**Estoy bien.**" Use "**yo soy**" when you are telling your profession, religion or gender. Test

yourself – write each sentence on the next page for more practice. Add your own personal

variations as well.

_____ ¿ _____ **cuesta esto?**
(how much)   (how much)   this *(es-toh)*

☐	**largo** *(lar-goh)*	long	_____
☐	**el latín** *(lah-teen)*	Latin	_____
☐	**la lección** *(lek-see-ohn)*	lesson	_____
☐	**legal** *(leh-gahl)*	legal	_____
☐	**el licor** *(lee-kor)*	liquor	_____

1

Yo soy católico. *(kah-toh-lee-koh)* _____
I am Catholic (♱)

Soy protestante. *(proh-tes-tahn-teh)* _____

Soy judío. *(hoo-dee-oh)* _____
Jewish (♱)

Soy americano. *(ah-mair-ee-kah-noh)* _____
American (♱)

Yo estoy en Europa. *(eh-oo-roh-pah)* _____

Soy canadiense. *(kah-nah-dee-en-seh)* _____
Canadian

Estoy en la iglesia. *(ee-gleh-see-ah)* _____
I am in church

Estoy en Barcelona. _____

Soy católica. _____
Catholic (♀)

Estoy en Chile. _____

Estoy en el hotel. *(oh-tel)* _____

Estoy en el restaurante. _____

Yo tengo hambre. *(tehn-goh) (ahm-breh)* _____
I have hunger

Yo tengo sed. *(sed)* _____
I have thirst

To negate any of these statements, simply add "**no**" before the verb.
not/no

No soy protestante. _____
I am not

No tengo sed. _____
I am not thirsty

Go through and drill these sentences again but with "**no.**"

Ahora, take a piece of paper. Our **familia** *(fah-mee-lee-ah)* from earlier had a reunion. Identify everyone

below by writing **la palabra** *(pah-lah-brah)* **española correcta** *(koh-rrek-tah)* for each person — **la madre, el tío** and so on.
correct

Don't forget **el perro!** *(peh-rroh)*

❏	**el limón** *(lee-mohn)*	lemon
❏	**la limonada** *(lee-moh-nah-dah)*	lemonade
❏	**la lista** *(lees-tah)*	list
❏	**el litro** *(lee-troh)*	liter
❏	**local** *(loh-kahl)*	local

1

_____
_____
_____
_____

¡Aprender! *(ah-pren-dair)* to learn

You have already used **dos** *(dohs)* very important verbs: **yo** (I) **quiero** *(kee-eh-roh)* (want) and **yo** (I) **tengo** *(tehn-goh)* (have). Although you might be able to get by with only these verbs, let's assume you want to do better. First a quick review.

How do you say **"I"** en **español?** *(es-pahn-yol)* ____________

How do you say **"we"** en **español?** ____________

Compare these **dos** *(dohs)* (two) charts **muy** *(mwee)* (very) carefully **y** learn these **siete** *(see-eh-teh)* (seven) **palabras** now.

I	=	**yo** *(yoh)* ____________
you	=	**usted** *(oos-ted)* ____________
he	=	**él** ____________
she	=	**ella** *(eh-yah)* ____________
we	=	**nosotros** *(noh-soh-trohs)* ____________
they	=	**ellos** *(eh-yohs)* (♂ or mixed) ____________
they	=	**ellas** *(eh-yahs)* (♀) ____________

Not too hard, is it? Draw lines between the matching **palabras inglesas y españolas** below to see if you can keep these **palabras** straight in your mind.

nosotros *(noh-soh-trohs)*	I
ellos *(eh-yohs)*	they (♀)
él	you
yo	he
usted *(oos-ted)*	we
ella *(eh-yah)*	she
ellas *(eh-yahs)*	they (♂)

- ❒ **mágico** *(mah-hee-koh)* .... magic ____________
- ❒ **el mapa** *(mah-pah)* .... map ____________
- ❒ **la marca** *(mar-kah)* .... mark **m** ____________
- ❒ **marzo** *(mar-soh)* .... March ____________
- ❒ **masculino** *(mahs-koo-lee-noh)* .... masculine ____________

Ahora close **el libro y** write out both columns of this practice on a piece of *(pah-pel)* **papel.** How did
paper

usted do? *(bee-en)* *(mahl)* **Bien o mal? Ahora** that **usted** know these **palabras, usted** can say almost anything
good or bad you you

en español with one basic formula: the "plug-in" formula.

To demonstrate, let's take *(sehs)* **seis** basic **y** practical verbs **y** see how the "plug-in" formula works.
six

Write the verbs in the blanks after **usted** have practiced saying them out loud many times.

(neh-seh-see-tar)
necesitar _____
to need

(ahn-dar)
andar _____
to walk, to go

(veh-neer)
venir ___venir, venir, venir___
to come

(keh-rair)
querer _____
to want

(ah-pren-dair)
aprender _____
to learn

(teh-nair)
tener _____
to have

Besides the familiar words already circled, can **usted** find the above verbs in the puzzle below?

When **usted** find them, write them in the blanks to the right.

A	R	O	H	A	F	I	J	Y	T	N
N	E	C	E	S	I	T	A	R	E	Ó
D	T	D	U	O	Q	U	I	É	N	C
A	P	R	E	N	D	E	R	Y	E	E
R	N	M	E	Q	U	E	R	E	R	U
O	R	D	U	Y	U	T	S	E	I	S
V	E	N	I	R	L	É	B	I	E	L
Y	O	Á	T	S	E	D	Ó	N	D	E

1. _____

2. _____

3. _____

4. _____

5. _____

6. _____

40

Study the following patterns carefully.

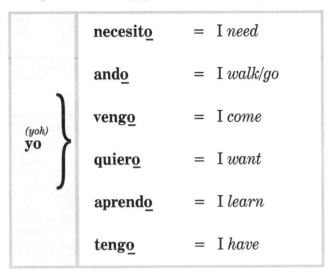
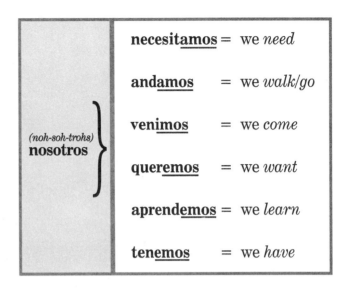

(yoh) **yo**	**necesito**	= I *need*	(noh-soh-trohs) **nosotros**	**necesitamos**	= we *need*
	ando	= I *walk/go*		**andamos**	= we *walk/go*
	vengo	= I *come*		**venimos**	= we *come*
	quiero	= I *want*		**queremos**	= we *want*
	aprendo	= I *learn*		**aprendemos**	= we *learn*
	tengo	= I *have*		**tenemos**	= we *have*

Note: • With all these verbs, the first thing you do is drop the final "**ar**," "**er**," or "**ir**" from the basic verb form or stem.

• With "**yo**," add "**o**" to the basic verb form.

• With "**nosotros**," add the vowel of the original ending plus "**mos**."

Some verbs just will not conform to the pattern! But don't worry. Speak slowly **y** clearly, **y** you will be perfectly understood whether you say "**yo veno**" or "**yo vengo**." Spanish speakers will be delighted that you have taken the time to learn their language.

Note: • Spanish has four separate and very different ways of saying "you" whereas in English we only use one word.

• "**Usted**" will be used throughout this book and will be appropriate for most situations. "**Usted**" refers to one person in a formal sense. "**Usted**" is abbreviated "**Ud.**"
you

• "**Ustedes**," abbreviated "**Uds**," refers to more than one person in a formal sense, as
you (plural)
we might say, "you all."

• "**Tú**" and its plural form "**vosotros**," are forms of address usually reserved for
(too)   (voh-soh-trohs)
you (singular)   you (plural)
family members and very close friends.

☐ **el medio** (*meh-dee-oh*)	middle	
☐ **el mediterráneo** (*meh-dee-teh-rrah-neh-oh*) . .	Mediterranean	
☐ **la melodía** (*meh-loh-dee-ah*)	melody	**m**
☐ **el menú** (*meh-noo*)	menu	
☐ **México** (*meh-hee-koh*)	Mexico	

Here's your next group of patterns!

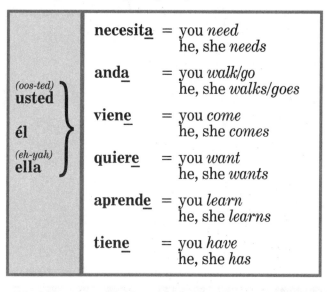
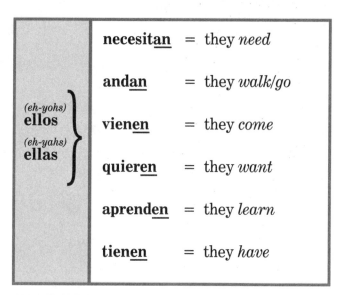

(oos-ted) **usted** **él** **(eh-yah)** **ella**	**necesit<u>a</u>** = you *need* he, she *needs*
	and<u>a</u> = you *walk/go* he, she *walks/goes*
	vien<u>e</u> = you *come* he, she *comes*
	quier<u>e</u> = you *want* he, she *wants*
	aprend<u>e</u> = you *learn* he, she *learns*
	tien<u>e</u> = you *have* he, she *has*

(eh-yohs) **ellos** **(eh-yahs)** **ellas**	**necesit<u>an</u>** = they *need*
	and<u>an</u> = they *walk/go*
	vien<u>en</u> = they *come*
	quier<u>en</u> = they *want*
	aprend<u>en</u> = they *learn*
	tien<u>en</u> = they *have*

Note: • Again drop the final "**ar**," "**er**," or "**ir**" from the basic verb form or stem.

• With "**usted**," "**él**" and "**ella**," add "**a**" if the original ending was "**ar**," and "**e**" for all others.

• With "**ellos**," and "**ellas**" simply add "**n**" to the "**usted**," "**él**" and "**ella**" form.

Aquí **están** **seis** more verbs.
here   are   *(sehs)* six

(kohm-prar)
comprar _____
to buy

(en-trar)
entrar _____
to enter

(vee-veer)
vivir _____
to live

(ah-blar)
hablar _____
to speak

(deh-seer)
decir _____
to say

(peh-deer)
pedir _____
to order, to request

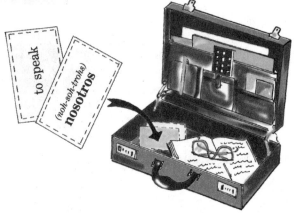

At the back of **el libro**, **usted** will find twelve

(pah-hee-nahs)
páginas of flash cards to help you learn these
pages

(nweh-vahs)
palabras nuevas. Cut them out; carry them in
new

your briefcase, purse, pocket **o** knapsack; **y**
(oh) or

review them whenever **usted** have a free moment.

☐ **el metro** *(meh-troh)* . . . . meter, metro (subway) _____
☐ **metropolitano** *(meh-troh-poh-lee-tah-noh)* . . metropolitan _____
☐ **el ministro** *(mee-nees-troh)* . . . . minister (government) _____
☐ **el minuto** *(mee-noo-toh)* . . . . minute _____
☐ **moderno** *(moh-dair-noh)* . . . . modern   **m**

42

Ahora, it is your turn to practice what **usted** have learned. Fill in the following blanks with the correct form of the verb. Each time **usted** write out the sentence, be sure to say it aloud.

(neh-seh-see-tar)
necesitar
to need

Yo _____ *(vah-soh)* *(ah-gwah)* un vaso de agua.
glass water

Usted _____ *(sair-veh-sah)* una cerveza.
beer

Él _____ *(vee-noh)* un vaso de vino.
Ella wine

Nosotros _____ *(tah-sahs)* *(teh)* dos tazas de té.
cups tea

Ellos _____ *(kah-feh)* tres tazas de café.
Ellas

(ahn-dar)
andar
to walk, to go

Yo _____ *(kah-sah)* a la casa.

Usted _____ *(plah-yah)* a la playa.
beach

Él _____ *(a+el)* *(oh-tel)* al hotel.
Ella

Nosotros _____ *(bahn-koh)* al banco.

Ellos _____ *(sair-vee-see-ohs)* a los servicios.
Ellas restrooms

(veh-neer)
venir
to come

Yo _____ *(meh-hee-koh)* de México.
from

Usted _____ *(ee-tah-lee-ah)* de Italia.

Él _viene/_ *(kah-nah-dah)* de Canadá.
Ella

Nosotros _____ de Inglaterra.

Ellos _____ de España.
Ellas

(keh-rair)
querer
to want

Yo _____ *(teen-toh)* un vaso de vino tinto.
red

Usted _____ *(blahn-koh)* un vaso de vino blanco.
white

Él _____ *(roh-sah-doh)* un vaso de vino rosado.
Ella rosé

Nosotros _____ *(ah-gwah)* tres vasos de agua.
water

Ellos _____ *(hoo-goh)* cinco vasos de jugo.
Ellas juice

(ah-pren-dair)
aprender
to learn

Yo _____ el español.

Usted _____ *(een-gles)* el inglés.

Él _____ *(ah-leh-mahn)* el alemán.
Ella German

Nosotros _____ *(frahn-ses)* el francés.
French

Ellos _____ *(chee-noh)* el chino.
Ellas Chinese

(teh-nair)
tener
to have

Yo _____ *(peh-sohs)* doscientos pesos.

Usted _tiene/_ dos mil pesos.

Él _____ *(doh-lar-es)* diez dólares americanos.
Ella

Nosotros _____ pesos.

Ellos _____ dólares.
Ellas

- ☐ **el momento** *(moh-men-toh)* .... moment
- ☐ **la monarquía** *(moh-nar-kee-ah)* .... monarchy
- ☐ **el monasterio** *(moh-nahs-teh-ree-oh)* .... monastery
- ☐ **la montaña** *(mohn-tahn-yah)* .... mountain
- ☐ **la música** *(moo-see-kah)* .... music

m _____
_____
_____

Now take a break, walk around the room, take a deep breath **y** do the next **seis** verbs.

(kohm-prar)
comprar
to buy

Yo _____ un **libro.** *(lee-broh)* book

Usted _____ un **reloj.** *(reh-loh)* watch/clock

Él _compra/_____ una **ensalada.**
Ella

Nosotros _____ un **automóvil.**

Ellos _____ dos **billetes** *(bee-yeh-tehs)* de **teatro.** *(teh-ah-troh)* theater
Ellas

(en-trar)
entrar
to enter

Yo _entro/_____ en el **hotel.** *(oh-tel)*

Usted _____ en el **banco.** *(bahn-koh)*

Él _____ en el **restaurante.**
Ella

Nosotros _____ en la **casa.** *(kah-sah)*

Ellos _____ en el **cuarto.** *(kwar-toh)* room
Ellas

(vee-veer)
vivir
to live

Yo _____ en los Estados **Unidos.** *(oo-nee-dohs)*

Usted _____ en **Europa.** *(ee-oo-roh-pah)*

Él _____ en **Canadá.** *(kah-nah-dah)*
Ella

Nosotros _vivimos/_____ en **México.**

Ellos _____ en **España.**
Ellas

(ah-blar)
hablar
to speak

¡Buenos días!

Yo _____ **español.**

Usted _____ **inglés.**

Él _____ **japonés.** *(hah-poh-nes)* Japanese
Ella

Nosotros _____ **francés.**

Ellos _hablan/_____ **portugués.** *(por-too-gwehs)* Portuguese
Ellas

(deh-seer)
decir
to say

¡Hola!

Yo _digo/_____ "**hola.**" *(oh-lah)* hi

Usted _dice/_____ "**sí.**" *(see)*

Él _dice/_____ "**no.**"
Ella

Nosotros _decimos/_____ "**adiós.**" *(ah-dee-ohs)*

Ellos no _dicen/_____ **nada.** *(nah-dah)* nothing
Ellas

(peh-deer)
pedir
to order, to request

Yo _pido/_____ un **vaso** de **agua.** *(ah-gwah)*

Usted _pide/_____ un **vaso** de **agua mineral.** *(mee-nair-ahl)*

Él _pide/_____ un **vaso** de **jugo** *(hoo-goh)* de **tomate.** *(toh-mah-teh)*
Ella

Nosotros _pedimos/_____ dos **vasos** de **leche.** *(leh-cheh)*

Ellos _piden/_____ tres **tazas** de **café.** *(tah-sahs)*
Ellas

☐ **la nación** *(nah-see-ohn)*	nation	
☐ **natural** *(nah-too-rahl)*	natural	**n** _____
☐ **necesario** *(neh-seh-sah-ree-oh)*	necessary	_____
☐ **negro** *(neh-groh)*	black	_____
☐ **no** *(noh)*	no, not	_____

Sí, *(see)* it is hard to get used to all those **palabras nuevas.** Just keep practicing **y** before **usted** know *yes*

it, **usted** will be using them naturally. **Ahora** is a perfect time to turn to the back of this **libro,**

clip out your verb flash cards **y** start flashing. Don't skip over your free **palabras** either. Check

them off in the box provided as **usted aprende** *(ah-pren-deh)* each one. See if **usted** can fill in the blanks
learn

below. **Las respuestas** *(res-pwehs-tahs)* are at the bottom of **la página.** *(pah-hee-nah)*
answers *page*

1. _____
(I speak Spanish.)

2. _____
(We learn Spanish.)

3. _____
(She needs ten pesos.)

4. _____
(He comes from the United States.)

5. _____
(They live in Canada.)

6. _____
(You buy a book.)

In the following Steps, **usted** will be intro-

duced to more verbs **y usted** should drill them

in exactly the same way as **usted** did in this

section. Look up **las palabras nuevas** in

your **diccionario** *(deek-see-oh-nah-ree-oh)* **y** make up your own
dictionary

sentences. Try out your **palabras nuevas** for

that's how you make them yours to use on

your holiday. Remember, the more **usted**

practice **ahora,** the more enjoyable your trip

will be. **¡Buena suerte!** *(bweh-nah) (swair-teh)*
good *luck*

13   *(keh)* *(oh-rah)*
¿Qué hora es?
what   time   is it

Usted know how to tell **los días de la** **semana** *(seh-mah-nah)* **y los** **meses del año,** *(meh-ses)* *(ahn-yoh)* so now let's learn to tell
days   week   months   year

time. As a traveler, **usted necesita** *(neh-seh-see-tah)* to be able to tell time in order to make **reservaciones,** *(reh-sair-vah-see-oh-nes)* **y**
reservations

to catch **trenes y autobuses. Aquí están** the "basics."
trains   buses   are

What time is it?	=	**¿Qué hora es?** *(oh-rah)* _____
	=	**¿Qué hora tiene usted?** *(tee-en-eh)* _____
		have you
minutes	=	**minutos** *(mee-noo-tohs)* _____
half past	=	**y media** *(ee) (meh-dee-ah)* _____
minus	=	**menos** *(meh-nohs)* _____
a quarter	=	**un cuarto** *(kwar-toh)* _____
a quarter before	=	**menos cuarto** _____
a quarter after	=	**y cuarto** _____

Ahora quiz yourself. Fill in the missing letters below.

minutes = | m | | n | | t | | s | minus = | m | e | | | s |

quarter before = | m | e | n | | s | ✕ | c | u | | r | t |

half past = | y | ✕ | | e | d | i | and finally

What time is it? | ¿ | Q | | é | ✕ | | o | | a | ✕ | | s | ? |

☐ **normal** *(nor-mahl)* . . . . normal   _____
☐ **el norte** *(nor-teh)* . . . . north   _____
☐ **la noticia** *(noh-tee-see-ah)* . . . . notice   **n**   _____
☐ **noviembre** *(noh-vee-em-breh)* . . . . November   _____
☐ **el número** *(noo-meh-roh)* . . . . number   _____

Ahora, cómo *(koh-moh)* are these **palabras** used? Study **los ejemplos** *(eh-hem-plohs)* **abajo** *(ah-bah-joh)*. When **usted** think it
how   examples   below

through, it really is not too difficult. Just notice that the pattern changes after the halfway mark.

Notice that the phrase "o'clock" is not used.

Son las cinco. *(seen-koh)*
it is   5 o'clock

5.00   Son las cinco. Son las cinco.

Son las cinco y diez. *(dee-es)*

5.10 _____

Son las cinco y cuarto. *(ee) (kwar-toh)*
and   a quarter

5.15 _____

Son las cinco y veinte. *(vain-teh)*

5.20 _____

Son las cinco y media.
half past five

5.30 _____

Son las seis menos veinte. *(sehs) (meh-nohs)*

5.40 _____

Son las seis menos cuarto.

5.45 _____

Son las seis menos diez.

5.50 _____

Son las seis.

6.00 _____

See how **importante** *(eem-por-tahn-teh)* learning **los números es**? Answer the following **preguntas** *(preh-goon-tahs)* based on **los**
                                                                                                    questions

relojes *(reh-loh-hes)* below.
clocks

1. 8.00 _____

2. 7.15 _____

3. 4.30 _____

4. 9.20 _____

47

When **usted** answer a "**¿Cuándo?**" question, say "**a**" before **usted** give the time.

when ... *at*

1. **¿Cuándo viene el tren?** _a las seis_
   (vee-en-eh)
   comes   train   (at 6:00)

2. **¿Cuándo viene el autobús?** _____
   comes   bus   (at 7:30)

3. **¿Cuándo comienza el concierto?** _____
   (koh-mee-en-sah)   (kohn-see-air-toh)
   begins/commences   concert   (at 8:00)

4. **¿Cuándo comienza la película?** _____
   (koh-mee-en-sah)   (peh-lee-koo-lah)
   begins   film   (at 9:00)

5. **¿Cuándo está abierto el restaurante?** _____
   (ah-bee-air-toh)
   is   open   (at 11:30)

6. **¿Cuándo está abierto el banco?** _____
   (bahn-koh)
   open   (at 8:30)

7. **¿Cuándo está cerrado el restaurante?** _____
   (seh-rrah-doh)
   closed   (at 5:30)

8. **¿Cuándo está cerrado el banco?** _____
   (at 10:30)

Aquí está a quick quiz. Fill in the blanks **con** the correct **números.**
(kohn) with

9. **Un minuto tiene** _____ **segundos.**
   (mee-noo-toh)   (seh-goon-dohs)
   minute   (?)   seconds

10. **Una hora tiene** _____ **minutos.**
    (oh-rah)   (mee-noo-tohs)
    hour   (?)   minutes

11. **Una semana tiene** _____ **días.**
    (seh-mah-nah)   (dee-ahs)
    week   (?)   days

12. **Un año tiene** _____ **meses.**
    (ahn-yoh)   (meh-ses)
    year   (?)   months

13. **Un año tiene** _____ **semanas.**
    (?)   weeks

14. **Un año tiene** _____ **días.**
    (?)

LAS RESPUESTAS

1. a las seis
2. a las siete y media
3. a las ocho
4. a las nueve
5. a las once y media
6. a las ocho y media
7. a las cinco y media
8. a las diez y media
9. sesenta
10. sesenta
11. siete
12. doce
13. cincuenta y dos
14. trescientos sesenta y cinco

Do **usted** remember your greetings from earlier? It is a good time to review them as they will

(mwee) *(eem-por-tahn-teh)*
always be **muy** **importante.**
very   important

(dee-seh)   *(bweh-nohs)* *(dee-ahs)* *(sehn-yoh-rah)*
A las ocho de la mañana uno dice, "¡ Buenos días, Señora Fernández!"
at   morning   says   good   morning

(key) *(deh-see-mohs)*
¿Qué decimos? _____ ¡Buenos días, Señora Fernández! _____
what   do we say

(bweh-nahs)   *(sehn-yor)*
A la una de la tarde uno dice, "¡Buenas tardes, Señor Valdes!"
one   afternoon

¿Qué decimos? _____

(noh-ches) *(sehn-yoh-ree-tah)*
A las ocho de la noche uno dice, "¡Buenas noches, Señorita Gallegos!"

¿Qué decimos? _____

(dee-es)   *(tahm-bee-en)*
A las diez de la noche uno dice también, "¡Buenas noches!"
ten   also   good   night

¿Qué decimos? _____

Usted have probably already noticed that plurals are generally formed by adding "s" (after a

vowel) or "es" (after a consonant).

(bee-see-kleh-tah)   *(bee-see-kleh-tahs)*
la bicicleta   **las bicicletas**
bicycle
(teh-leh-foh-noh)   *(teh-leh-foh-nohs)*
el teléfono   **los teléfonos**
(ow-toh-boos)   *(ow-toh-boo-ses)*
el autobús   **los autobuses**
bus

En español adjectives agree with the gender and number of the nouns they modify **y** they

generally come after the noun (but not always!)

(roh-hah)   *(roh-hahs)*
la bicicleta roja   **las bicicletas rojas**
red
(neh-groh)   *(neh-grohs)*
el teléfono negro   **los teléfonos negros**
black
(vair-deh)
el autobús verde   **los autobuses verdes**
green

- ☐ **el objeto** *(ohb-heh-toh)* . . . . object _____
- ☐ **la ocasión** *(oh-kah-see-ohn)* . . . . occasion _____
- ☐ **la oliva** *(oh-lee-vah)* . . . . olive   **o** _____
- ☐ **la ópera** *(oh-peh-rah)* . . . . opera _____
- ☐ **oriental** *(oh-ree-en-tahl)* . . . . oriental _____

Aquí están the new verbs for Step 13.

(koh-mair)
comer _____

to eat

(beh-bair)
beber _____

to drink

(koh-mair)
comer
to eat

(beh-bair)
beber
to drink

Yo _____ *(en-sah-lah-dah)* **la ensalada.**

Usted *come/* _____ *(soh-pah)* **la sopa.**
soup

(moo-choh)
Él _____ **mucho.**
Ella a lot

Nosotros _____ *(pahn)* **el pan.**
bread

(nah-dah)
Ellos no _____ **nada.**
Ellas nothing

Yo _____ *(leh-cheh)* **leche.**
milk

(nah-dah)
Usted no _____ **nada.**
nothing

(lee-moh-nah-dah)
Él *bebe/* _____ **limonada.**
Ella

Nosotros _____ **café.**

Ellos _____ **té.**
Ellas

Usted have learned that to negate a statement, simply add **no** before the verb. Notice in the

(nah-dah)
examples above, that when you used the word "**nada**," you also added "**no**" before the verb.
nothing

(dee-goh)		
Yo no digo nada.		**No digo nada.**
say nothing		
(kohm-prah-mohs)	OR	
Nosotros no compramos nada.		**No compramos nada.**
we buy nothing		

- ☐ **el occidente** *(ohk-see-den-teh)* . . . . occident, west _____
- ☐ **el océano** *(oh-seh-ah-noh)* . . . . ocean _____
- ☐ **ocupado** *(oh-koo-pah-doh)* . . . . occupied **O** _____
- ☐ **la oficina** *(oh-fee-see-nah)* . . . . office _____
- ☐ **la operación** *(oh-peh-rah-see-ohn)* . . . . operation _____

Usted have learned a lot of material in the last few steps **y** that means it is time to quiz yourself. Don't panic, this is just for you **y** no one else needs to know how **usted** did. Remember, this is a chance to review, find out, what **usted** remember **y** what **usted necesita** to spend more time on. After **usted** have finished, check your **respuestas** in the glossary at the back of this book. Circle the correct answers.

café -	tea	coffee	**familia -**	seven	family
sí -	yes	no	**niños -**	children	grandfather
tía -	aunt	uncle	**leche -**	butter	(milk)
o -	and	or	**sal -**	pepper	salt
aprender -	to drink	to learn	**abajo -**	under	over
noche -	morning	night	**hombre -**	man	doctor
martes -	Friday	Tuesday	**junio -**	June	July
hablar -	to live	to speak	**cocina -**	kitchen	religions
verano -	summer	winter	**tengo -**	I want	I have
dinero -	money	page	**comprar -**	to order	to buy
diez -	nine	ten	**ayer -**	yesterday	tomorrow
mucho -	a lot	bread	**bueno -**	good	yellow

¿Cómo está?   <u>What time is it?</u>   <u>How are you?</u>   Well, how are you after this quiz?

☐ **la oportunidad** *(oh-por-too-nee-dahd)* . . . . opportunity
☐ **la oposición** *(oh-poh-see-see-ohn)* . . . . opposition
☐ **ordinario** *(or-dee-nah-ree-oh)* . . . . ordinary   **O**
☐ **original** *(oh-ree-hee-nahl)* . . . . original
☐ **el oxígeno** *(ohk-see-heh-noh)* . . . . oxygen

_____
_____
_____
_____
_____

(nor-teh) *(soor)* *(es-teh)* *(oh-es-teh)*
Norte - Sur, Este - Oeste
north   south   east   west

If **usted** are looking at **un mapa** *(mah-pah)* **y usted** see the following **palabras,** it should not be too
map

difficult to figure out what they mean. Take an educated guess.

(ah-meh-ree-kah) *(nor-teh)* **América del Norte**

(ah-meh-ree-kah) *(soor)* **América del Sur**

(poh-loh) **Polo Norte**

(poh-loh) **Polo Sur**

(koh-stah) *(es-teh)* **la costa del este**

(koh-stah) *(oh-es-teh)* **la costa del oeste**

(eer-lahn-dah) **Irlanda del Norte**

(ah-free-kah) **Africa del Sur**

Las palabras españolas para "north," "south," "east," **y** "west" are easy to recognize due to

their similarity to **inglés.** These **palabras son muy importantes.** Learn them **hoy!**
(sohn)(mwee) *(oy)*
are

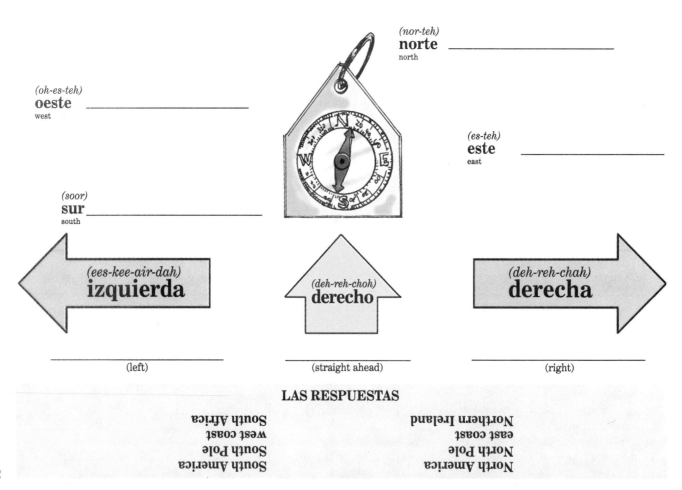

(nor-teh) **norte** _____
north

(oh-es-teh) **oeste** _____
west

(es-teh) **este** _____
east

(soor) **sur** _____
south

(ees-kee-air-dah) **izquierda**

(deh-reh-choh) **derecho**

(deh-reh-chah) **derecha**

_____ (left)

_____ (straight ahead)

_____ (right)

LAS RESPUESTAS

South Africa | Northern Ireland
west coast | east coast
South Pole | North Pole
South America | North America

These **palabras** can go a long way. Say them aloud each time you write them in the blanks below.

(por) (fah-vor)
por favor _____
please

(grah-see-ahs)
gracias _____
thank you

(pair-doh-neh-meh) (pair-dohn)
perdóneme / perdón _____
excuse me

(deh) (nah-dah)
de nada _____
you're welcome

(kohn-vair-sah-see-oh-nes) (mwee) (tee-pee-kahs)(pah-rah)
Aquí están dos conversaciones   muy   típicas   para someone who is trying to find something.
two   conversations   very typical for

Write them out in the blanks below.

Juan:
(pair-doh-neh-meh)   *(ah-kah-pool-koh)*
Perdóneme. ¿Dónde está el Hotel Acapulco?
excuse me

_____ *Perdóneme. ¿Dónde está el Hotel Acapulco?* _____

Carlos:
(vah-yah)   (dohs) (kah-yes) (mahs) (doh-bleh)   (ees-kee-air-dah)
Vaya usted dos calles más y doble usted a la izquierda.
go   streets more   turn   to the left

_____

(deh-reh-chah)
El Hotel Acapulco está a la derecha.
                          on   right

_____

Ricardo:
                                       (moo-seh-oh)   (ar-tes)
Perdóneme. ¿Dónde está el Museo de Artes?
                                        museum

_____

Cristina:
(vah-yah)   (deh-reh-chah) (lweh-goh) (deh-reh-choh) (ah-prohk-see-mah-dah-men-teh) (see-en) (meh-trohs)
Vaya usted a la derecha y luego derecho aproximadamente   cien metros.
go   then   straight ahead approximately   meters

_____

(ees-kee-air-dah)
El Museo está a la izquierda.
                      left

_____

❏ **el palacio** *(pah-lah-see-oh)* .... palace   _____
❏ **la palma** *(pahl-mah)* .... palm   _____
❏ **el pánico** *(pah-nee-koh)* .... panic   **p** _____
❏ **el pasaporte** *(pah-sah-por-teh)* .... passport   _____
❏ **la pasta** *(pahs-tah)* .... paste, pasta   _____

Are **usted** lost? There is no need to be lost if **usted** have learned the basic direction **palabras.**

Do not try to memorize these **conversaciones** *(kohn-vair-sah-see-oh-nes)* because **usted** will never be looking for

precisely these places. One day, **usted** might need to ask **direcciones** *(dee-rek-see-oh-nes)* to "El Hotel **Cervantes**" *(sair-vahn-tes)*
directions

or "El Restaurante del **Río**." *(ree-oh)* Learn the key direction **palabras y** be sure **usted** can find your
river

destination. **Usted** may want to buy a guidebook to start planning which places **usted** would like

to visit. Practice asking **direcciones** to these special places. What if the person responding to

your **pregunta** *(preh-goon-tah)* answers too quickly for **usted** to understand the entire reply? Practice saying,
question

Perdóneme. No comprendo. Repita usted eso, por favor.
    I do not understand   *(reh-pee-tah)*
                           repeat   that

Ahora, say it again **y** then write it out below.

_____

(Excuse me. I do not understand. Please repeat.)

Sí, es difícil *(see) (dee-fee-seel)* at first but don't give up! **Cuando** *(kwahn-doh)* the directions are repeated, **usted** will be able to
yes   difficult   when

understand if **usted** have learned the key **palabras.** Let's review by writing them in the blanks below.

right

_____
(north)

_____   _____
(west)   (east)

left

_____
(south)

❐	**la pausa** *(pow-sah)*	pause	_____
❐	**la pera** *(peh-rah)*	pear	_____
❐	**el perdón** *(pair-dohn)*	pardon	**p** _____
❐	**perfecto** *(pair-fek-toh)*	perfect	_____
❐	**el perfume** *(pair-foo-meh)*	perfume	_____

Aquí *(ah-ee)* **hay cuatro** verbs **nuevos.** *(nweh-vohs)*
are   new

(eer)
ir _____
to go

(kohm-pren-dair)
comprender _____
to understand

(ven-dair)
vender _____
to sell

(reh-peh-teer)
repetir _____
to repeat

As always, say each sentence out loud. Say each **y** every **palabra** carefully, pronouncing each sound **en español** as well as **usted** can. Remember, "**a** " *(ah)* plus "**el**" becomes " **al.**" *(ahl)*
to   the

(eer)
ir
to go

Yo __voy/_____ **al hotel.** *(oh-tel)*

Usted __va/_____ **al restaurante.** *(res-tow-rahn-teh)*

Él __va/_____ **al banco.** *(bahn-koh)*
Ella

Nosotros __vamos/_____ **al museo.** *(moo-seh-oh)*

Ellos __van/_____ **a la casa.**
Ellas

(kohm-pren-dair)
comprender
to understand

Yo __comprendo/_____ **el español.**

Usted _____ **el inglés.**

Él _____ **el alemán.** *(ah-leh-mahn)*
Ella   German

Nosotros _____ **el ruso.** *(roo-soh)*
                                                         Russian
Ellos _____ **el francés.** *(frahn-ses)*
Ellas   French

(ven-dair)
vender
to sell

Yo _____ **libros.** *(lee-brohs)*

Usted __vende/_____ **carros.** *(kah-rrohs)*
                                                         cars
Él _____ **tarjetas postales.** *(tar-heh-tahs) (pohs-tah-les)*
Ella   postcards

Nosotros _____ **billetes.** *(bee-yeh-tes)*

Ellos _____ **sellos.** *(say-yohs)*
Ellas   stamps

(reh-peh-teer)
repetir *Qué? Qué? Qué?*
to repeat

Yo __repito/_____ **la palabra.**

Usted _____ **las direcciones.**

Él __repite/_____ **el nombre.** *(nohm-breh)*
Ella

Nosotros __repetimos/_____ **la pregunta.** *(preh-goon-tah)*
                                                         question
Ellos no __repiten/_____ **nada.** *(nah-dah)*
Ellas   nothing

15

(ah-rree-bah) *(ah-bah-hoh)*
Arriba – Abajo
upstairs/up   downstairs/down

(ah-pren-deh-mohs) *(kah-sah)* *(seh-vee-yah)*
Ahora nosotros aprendemos más palabras. Aquí está una casa en Sevilla. Go to your
learn   more

(dor-mee-toh-ree-oh) *(kwar-toh)*
dormitorio y look around **el cuarto.** Let's learn the names of the things **en su dormitorio,**
bedroom   room

just like **nosotros** learned the various parts of **la casa.**

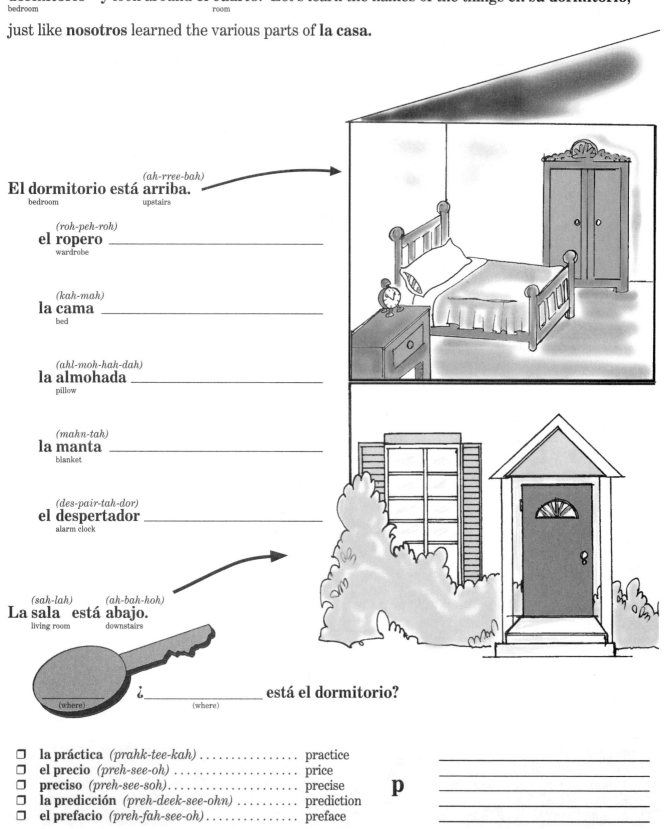

(ah-rree-bah)
El dormitorio está arriba.
bedroom   upstairs

(roh-peh-roh)
el ropero _____
wardrobe

(kah-mah)
la cama _____
bed

(ahl-moh-hah-dah)
la almohada _____
pillow

(mahn-tah)
la manta _____
blanket

(des-pair-tah-dor)
el despertador _____
alarm clock

(sah-lah) *(ah-bah-hoh)*
La sala está abajo.
living room   downstairs

_____
(where)

¿_____ está el dormitorio?
(where)

- ❏ **la práctica** *(prahk-tee-kah)* .... practice   _____
- ❏ **el precio** *(preh-see-oh)* .... price   _____
- ❏ **preciso** *(preh-see-soh)*..................... precise   **p**   _____
- ❏ **la predicción** *(preh-deek-see-ohn)* ...... prediction   _____
- ❏ **el prefacio** *(preh-fah-see-oh)*.............. preface   _____

Ahora, remove the next **cinco** stickers **y** label these things **en su dormitorio.** Let's move **al**

(bahn-yoh) *your* *(kwar-toh)*

baño y do the same thing. Remember, **el baño** means **un cuarto** to bathe in. If **usted está**

bathroom *room*

(neh-seh-see-tah) *(sair-vee-see-ohs)*

en el restaurante, y necesita to use the lavatory, **usted** want to ask for **los servicios o**

need *or*

(es-koo-sah-doh)

el excusado not for **el baño.** Restrooms may be marked with pictures **o** simply

or

with the letters **D** o **C.** Don't confuse them!

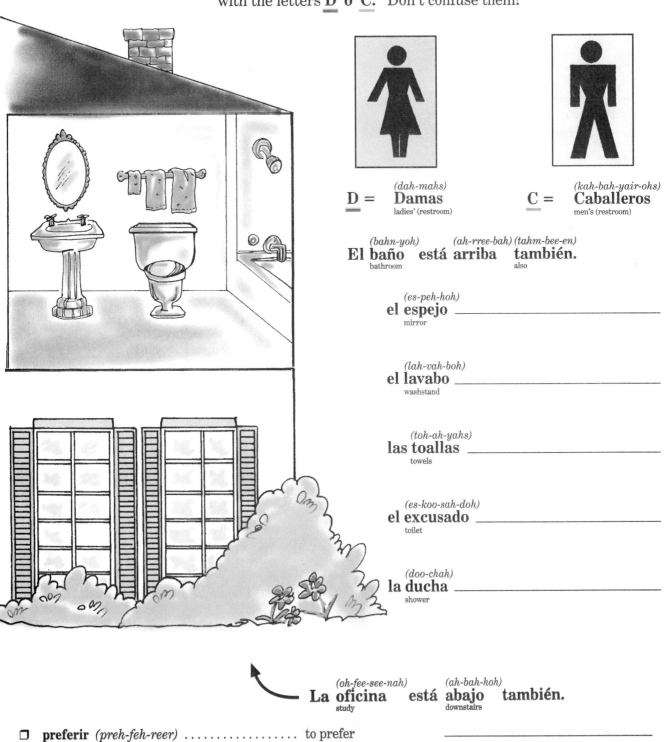

(dah-mahs)

D = Damas

ladies' (restroom)

(kah-bah-yair-ohs)

C = Caballeros

men's (restroom)

(bahn-yoh) *(ah-rree-bah)* *(tahm-bee-en)*

El baño está arriba también.

bathroom *also*

(es-peh-hoh)

el espejo _____

mirror

(lah-vah-boh)

el lavabo _____

washstand

(toh-ah-yahs)

las toallas _____

towels

(es-koo-sah-doh)

el excusado _____

toilet

(doo-chah)

la ducha _____

shower

(oh-fee-see-nah) *(ah-bah-hoh)*

La oficina está abajo también.

study *downstairs*

❏ **preferir** *(preh-feh-reer)* . . . . to prefer   _____

❏ **preparar** *(preh-pah-rar)* . . . . to prepare   _____

❏ **presente** *(preh-sen-teh)* . . . . present   **p** _____

❏ **principal** *(preen-see-pahl)* . . . . principal, main _____

❏ **probable** *(proh-bah-bleh)* . . . . probable _____

No forget to remove the next group of stickers **y** label these things in your *(bahn-yoh)* **baño.** Okay, it is time to review. Here's a quick quiz to see what you remember.

men's (restroom)

I understand

downstairs

please

towels

upstairs

bathroom

lavatory/restroom

straight ahead

women's (restroom)

(ah-bah-hoh)
abajo

(kah-bah-yair-ohs)
caballeros

(fah-vor)
por favor

(kohm-pren-doh)
yo comprendo

(sair-vee-see-ohs)
los servicios

(deh-reh-choh)
derecho

(dah-mahs)
damas

(toh-ah-yahs)
las toallas

(ah-rree-bah)
arriba

(bahn-yoh)
el baño

❏ **el problema** *(proh-bleh-mah)* . . . . problem
❏ **el producto** *(proh-dook-toh)* . . . . product
❏ **el profesor** *(proh-feh-sor)* . . . . professor   **p**
❏ **el programa** *(proh-grah-mah)* . . . . program
❏ **prohibido** *(proh-hee-bee-doh)* . . . . prohibited, forbidden

Next stop — **la oficina,** *(oh-fee-see-nah)* office specifically **la mesa** *(meh-sah)* table **o el escritorio** *(es-kree-toh-ree-oh)* desk **en la oficina. ¿Qué está**

sobre el escritorio? on Let's identify **las cosas** *(koh-sahs)* things which one normally finds **sobre el escritorio** or

strewn about **la oficina.**

(teh-leh-vee-sor)
el televisor
television

(lah-pees)
el lápiz
pencil

(ploo-mah)
la pluma
pen

(kohm-poo-tah-dor-ah)
la computadora
computer

(pah-pel)
el papel
paper

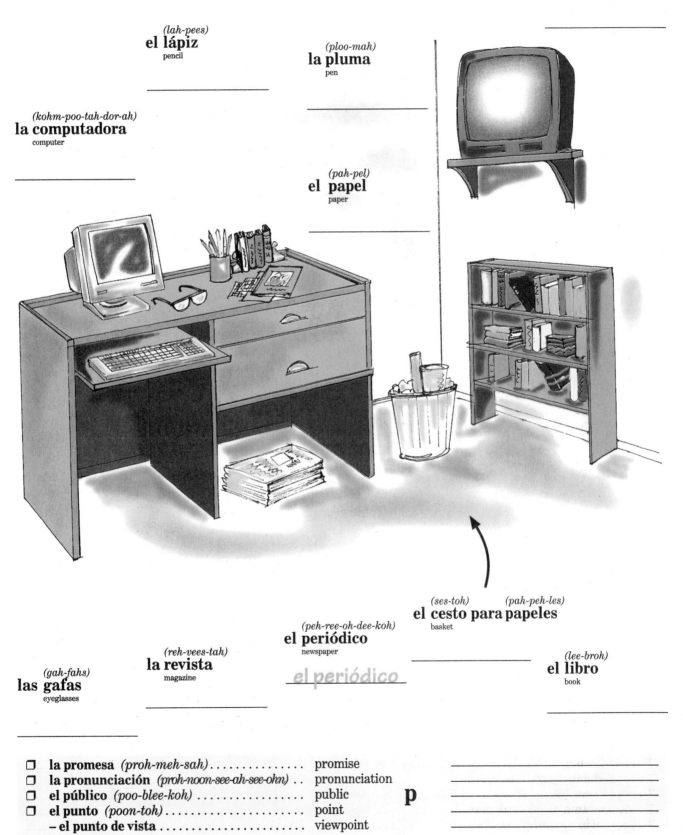

(ses-toh) *(pah-peh-les)*
el cesto para papeles
basket

(peh-ree-oh-dee-koh)
el periódico
newspaper

(reh-vees-tah)
la revista
magazine

(gah-fahs)
las gafas
eyeglasses

el periódico

(lee-broh)
el libro
book

p

Don't forget these essentials!

(kar-tah)
la carta
letter

(say-yoh)
el sello
stamp

(tar-heh-tah) (pohs-tahl)
la tarjeta   postal
postcard

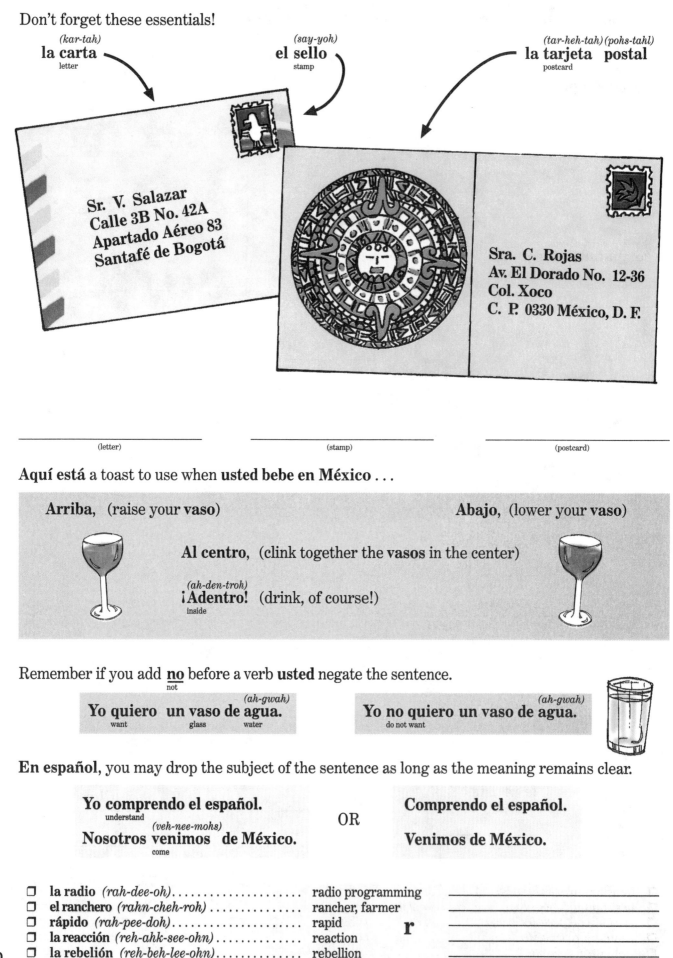

Sr. V. Salazar
Calle 3B No. 42A
Apartado Aéreo 83
Santafé de Bogotá

Sra. C. Rojas
Av. El Dorado No. 12-36
Col. Xoco
C. P. 0330 México, D. F.

_____   _____   _____
(letter)   (stamp)   (postcard)

Aquí está a toast to use when **usted bebe en México** . . .

Arriba, (raise your **vaso**)   **Abajo,** (lower your **vaso**)

Al centro, (clink together the **vasos** in the center)

(ah-den-troh)
¡Adentro! (drink, of course!)
inside

Remember if you add **<u>no</u>** before a verb **usted** negate the sentence.
          not

(ah-gwah)
Yo quiero un vaso de agua.
want   glass   water

(ah-gwah)
Yo no quiero un vaso de agua.
do not want

En español, you may drop the subject of the sentence as long as the meaning remains clear.

Yo comprendo el español.
understand
(veh-nee-mohs)
Nosotros venimos de México.
come

OR

Comprendo el español.

Venimos de México.

❏ **la radio** *(rah-dee-oh)*	radio programming	_____
❏ **el ranchero** *(rahn-cheh-roh)*	rancher, farmer	_____
❏ **rápido** *(rah-pee-doh)*	rapid	**r** _____
❏ **la reacción** *(reh-ahk-see-ohn)*	reaction	_____
❏ **la rebelión** *(reh-beh-lee-ohn)*	rebellion	_____

Simple, isn't it? **Ahora,** after you fill in the blanks below, go back a second time and negate all

these sentences by adding **"<u>no</u>"** before each verb. Then go back a third time **y** drop the subject.

Don't get discouraged! Just look at how much **usted** have already learned **y** think ahead to

(tah-pahs)
tapas, wonderful scenery **y** new adventures.
snacks

(vair)
ver _____
to see

(dor-meer)
dormir _____
to sleep

(mahn-dar)
mandar _____
to send

(yah-mar)
llamar _____
to phone, to call

(vair)
<u>ver</u>
to see

Yo _veol_____ *(mair-kah-doh)* **el mercado.**
market

Usted _vel_____ *(moo-seh-oh)* **el Museo de Artes.**

Él _____ *(pah-lah-see-oh) (nah-see-oh-nahl)* **el Palacio Nacional.**
Ella   National Palace

Nosotros _vemos/_ *(meh-dee-tair-rah-neh-oh)* **el Mar Mediterráneo.**
                                               Mediterranean Sea

Ellos _ven/_____ *(mohn-tahn-yahs)* **las montañas.**
Ellas   mountains

(mahn-dar)
<u>mandar</u>
to send

Yo _____ **la carta.**
letter

Usted _____ **la tarjeta postal.**

Él _manda/_____ **el libro.**
Ella

Nosotros _____ **dos tarjetas postales.**

Ellos _____ **cinco cartas.**
Ellas

(dor-meer)
<u>dormir</u>
to sleep

Yo _duermo/_____ **en el dormitorio.**
bedroom

Usted _____ **en el hotel.**

Él _duerme/_____ **en la casa.**
Ella

Nosotros _dormimos/_ *(deh-bah-hoh)* **debajo de la manta.**
                                     under   blanket

Ellos _duermen/_ *(seen) (ahl-moh-hah-dahs)* **sin las almohadas.**
Ellas   without   pillows

(yah-mar)
<u>llamar</u>
to phone, to call

Yo _____ **por teléfono.**

Usted _____ *(es-tah-dohs) (oo-nee-dohs)* **a los Estados Unidos.**
                                                   U.S.A.

Él _____ *(ee-tah-lee-ah)* **a Italia.**
Ella

Nosotros _llamamos/_ *(een-glah-teh-rrah)* **a Inglaterra.**
                                           England
                                           (kah-nah-dah)
Ellos _____ **a Canadá.**
Ellas

☐ **recibir** *(reh-see-beer)* . . . . to receive
☐ **regular** *(reh-goo-lar)* . . . . regular
☐ **la relación** *(reh-lah-see-ohn)* . . . . relation
☐ **la religión** *(reh-lee-hee-ohn)* . . . . religion
☐ **el remite** *(reh-mee-teh)* . . . . return address

r _____
_____
_____
_____
_____

Before **usted** proceed with the next step, **por favor** identify all the items **abajo**.

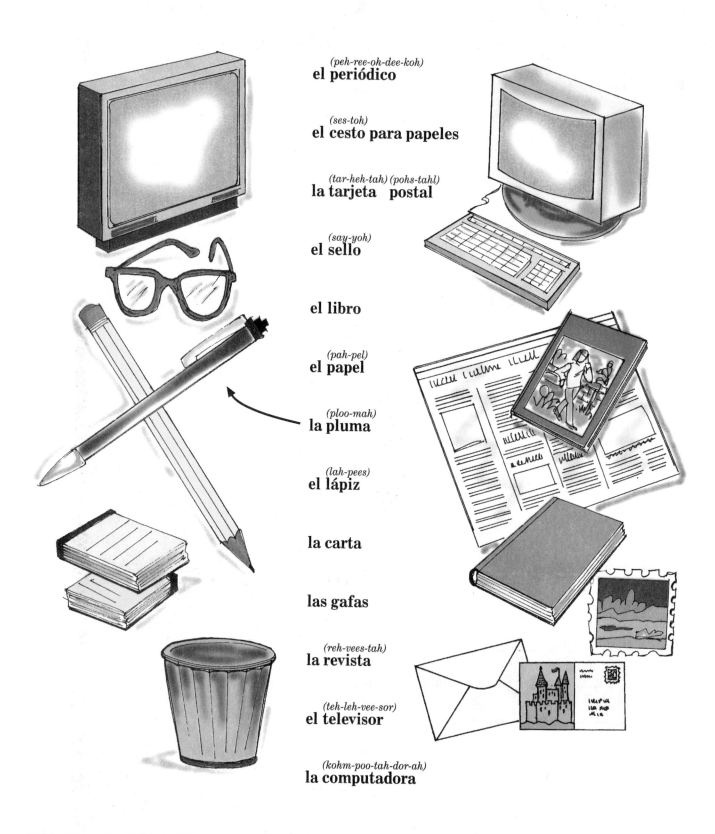

(peh-ree-oh-dee-koh)
el periódico

(ses-toh)
el cesto para papeles

(tar-heh-tah) (pohs-tahl)
la tarjeta   postal

(say-yoh)
el sello

el libro

(pah-pel)
el papel

(ploo-mah)
la pluma

(lah-pees)
el lápiz

la carta

las gafas

(reh-vees-tah)
la revista

(teh-leh-vee-sor)
el televisor

(kohm-poo-tah-dor-ah)
la computadora

❏	**reparar** *(reh-pah-rar)*	to repair	
❏	**repetir** *(reh-peh-teer)*	to repeat	
	– Repita por favor	please repeat	**r**
❏	**la república** *(reh-poo-blee-kah)*	republic	
❏	**la reserva** *(reh-sair-vah)*	reservation	

Ahora usted know how to count, how to ask **preguntas,** *(preh-goon-tahs)* how to use verbs **con** *(kohn)* the "plug-in"
questions

formula **y** how to describe something, be it the location of **un hotel o el color de una casa.** *(kah-sah)* Let's
house

take the basics that **usted** have learned **y** expand them in special areas that will be most helpful

in your travels. What does everyone do on a holiday? Send **tarjetas postales,** of course! Let's

learn exactly how **la oficina de correos** *(koh-rreh-ohs)* works.
post office

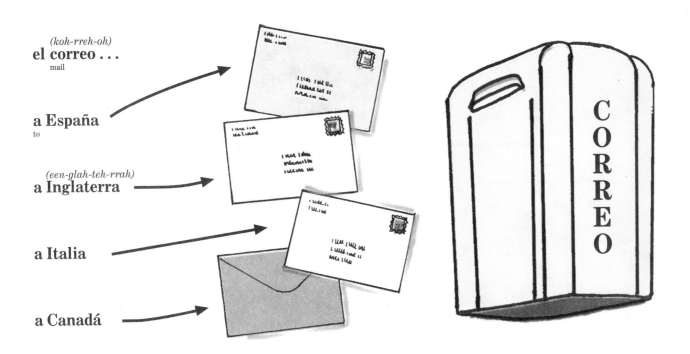

(koh-rreh-oh)
el correo . . .
mail

a España
to

(een-glah-teh-rrah)
a Inglaterra

a Italia

a Canadá

La oficina de correos is where **usted** buy **sellos,** *(say-yohs)* send **paquetes,** *(pah-keh-tes)* **cartas y tarjetas postales.**
packages

In large cities, **usted** can send **telegramas** *(teh-leh-grah-mahs)* or make **llamadas** *(yah-mah-dahs)* **de larga distancia** *(dees-tahn-see-ah)* **o**
telegrams   long-distance calls

llamadas internacionales *(yah-mah-dahs) (een-tair-nah-see-oh-nah-les)* **en la oficina de correos. La oficina de correos** frequently

tiene una ventanilla *(ven-tah-nee-yah)* which is open late **y** on Saturdays.
window/counter

❏	**el restaurante** *(res-tow-rahn-teh)*	restaurant		_____
❏	**la revolución** *(reh-voh-loo-see-ohn)*	revolution	**r**	_____
❏	**romano** *(roh-mah-noh)*	Roman		_____
❏	**romántico** *(roh-mahn-tee-koh)*	romantic	**s**	_____
❏	**la sal** *(sahl)*	salt		_____

Aquí están the necessary **palabras para la oficina de correos.** Practice them aloud y write them in the blanks.

(kar-tah)
la carta
letter

(tar-heh-tah) (pohs-tahl)
la tarjeta   postal
postcard

_____

_____

(pah-keh-teh)
el paquete
package

(teh-leh-grah-mah)
el telegrama
telegram

_____

_____

(koh-rreh-oh) (ah-eh-reh-oh)
correo   aéreo
by airmail

(fahks)
el fax

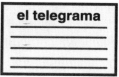

_____

_____

(say-yoh)
el sello
stamp

(kah-bee-nah)   (teh-leh-foh-noh)
la cabina   de teléfono
telephone booth

_____

_____

(boo-sohn)
el buzón
mailbox

(teh-leh-foh-noh)
el teléfono

_____

_____

- ☐ **el salario** *(sah-lah-ree-oh)* . . . . salary
- ☐ **el salmón** *(sahl-mohn)* . . . . salmon
- ☐ **el santo** *(sahn-toh)* . . . . saint
- ☐ **la sardina** *(sar-dee-nah)* . . . . sardine
- ☐ **el secretario** *(seh-kreh-tah-ree-oh)* . . . . secretary

S

_____
_____
_____
_____
_____

Next step — **usted** ask **preguntas** *(preh-goon-tahs)* like those **abajo,** depending on what **usted quiere.** *(kee-eh-reh)* Repeat
these sentences aloud many times.

¿Dónde compro sellos? *(dohn-deh) (kohm-proh) (say-yohs)* _____
do I buy

¿Dónde compro una tarjeta postal? *(kohm-proh) (tar-heh-tah)(pohs-tahl)* _____

¿Dónde hay un teléfono? *(ah-ee)* _____
is there

¿Dónde hay un buzón? *(ah-ee) (boo-sohn)* _____
is there   mailbox

¿Dónde hay una cabina de teléfono? *(ah-ee) (kah-bee-nah)* _____
public telephone

¿Dónde puedo mandar un paquete? *(pweh-doh) (mahn-dar) (pah-keh-teh)* _____
can I

¿Dónde puedo hacer una llamada local? *(pweh-doh) (ah-sair) (yah-mah-dah) (loh-kahl)* _____
make   call

¿Cuánto cuesta eso? *(kwes-tah) (eh-soh)* _¿Cuánto cuesta eso? ¿Cuánto cuesta eso?_____
costs

Ahora, quiz yourself. See if **usted** can translate the following thoughts into **español.** *(es-pahn-yohl)*

1. Where is a telephone booth? _____

2. Where can I phone to the U.S.A.? _____

3. Where can I make a local telephone call? _____

4. Where is the post office? _____

5. Where do I buy stamps? _____

6. Airmail stamps? _____

7. Where do I send a package? _____

8. Where do I send a fax? _____

LAS RESPUESTAS

1. ¿Dónde hay una cabina de teléfono?
2. ¿Dónde puedo llamar por teléfono a los Estados Unidos?
3. ¿Dónde puedo hacer una llamada local?
4. ¿Dónde está la oficina de correos?
5. ¿Dónde compro sellos?
6. ¿Sellos de correo aéreo?
7. ¿Dónde mando un paquete?
8. ¿Dónde mando un fax?

(ah-ee) *(vair-bohs)*
Aquí hay más verbos.
are   verbs

(ah-sair)
hacer _____
to make, to do

(dah-meh)
dame _____
give me

(es-kree-beer)
escribir _____
to write

(pah-gar)
pagar _____
to pay

Practice these verbs by not only filling in the blanks, but by saying them aloud many, many

times until you are comfortable with the sounds **y** the words.

(ah-sair)
hacer
to make, to do

(yah-mah-dah)
Yo __hago/_____ una llamada.
call

(loh-kahl)
Usted __hace/_____ una llamada local.

(moo-choh)
Él no _____ mucho.
Ella   a lot

Nosotros no _____ mucho.

(toh-doh)
Ellos _____ todo.
Ellas   everything

(es-kree-beer)
escribir
to write

(dee-rek-see-ohn)
Yo _____ la dirección.
address

(moo-choh)
Usted __escribe/_____ mucho.
a lot
(nah-dah)
Él no _____ nada.
Ella   nothing

Nosotros _____ dos cartas.

(soos) *(feer-mahs)*
Ellos _____ sus firmas.
Ellas   their signatures

(dah-meh)
dame
give me

(kwehn-tah)
__Dame/_____ la cuenta, por favor.
bill

_____ el menú, por favor.

(bee-yeh-teh)
_____ el billete, por favor.

(dee-rek-see-ohn)
_____ la dirección, por favor.

(nohm-breh)
_____ el nombre, por favor.

(pah-gar)
pagar
to pay

(kwehn-tah)
Yo __pago/_____ la cuenta.
bill
(teh-ah-troh)
Usted _____ los billetes de teatro.
theater

Él _____ los billetes de tren.
Ella

Nosotros _____ los billetes de museo.

(kohn-see-air-toh)
Ellos _____ los billetes de concierto.
Ellas   concert

☐ **la sensación** *(sen-sah-see-ohn)* .... sensation
☐ **septiembre** *(sep-tee-em-breh)* .... September
☐ **el servicio** *(sair-vee-see-oh)* .... service
☐ **la sesión** *(seh-see-ohn)* .... session
☐ **severo** *(seh-veh-roh)* .... severe

s

_____
_____
_____
_____

Some of these signs you probably recognize, but take a couple of minutes to review them anyway.

(kah-mee-noh) (seh-rrah-doh)
camino cerrado
road closed to vehicles

(ah-doo-ah-nah)
aduana
customs

(en-trar)
no entrar
no entrance

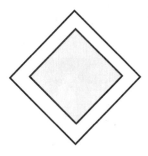

(kah-mee-noh)   (pree-or-ee-dahd)
camino con prioridad
main road, you have the right of way

(seh-dair) (pah-soh)
ceder el paso
yield

(lee-mee-teh)   (veh-loh-see-dahd)
límite de velocidad
speed limit

(es-tah-see-oh-nar)
no estacionar
no parking

(pah-sar)
no pasar
no passing

(pah-reh)(ahl-toh)
pare/ alto
stop

(des-vee-oh)
DESVÍO
detour

What follows are approximate conversions, so when you order something by liters, kilograms or grams you will have an idea of what to expect and not find yourself being handed one piece of candy when you thought you ordered an entire bag.

To Convert		Do the Math		
liters (l) to gallons,	multiply by 0.26	4 liters x 0.26	=	1.04 gallons
gallons to liters,	multiply by 3.79	10 gal. x 3.79	=	37.9 liters
kilograms (kg) to pounds,	multiply by 2.2	2 kilograms x 2.2	=	4.4 pounds
pounds to kilos,	multiply by 0.46	10 pounds x 0.46	=	4.6 kg
grams (g) to ounces,	multiply by 0.035	100 grams x 0.035	=	3.5 oz.
ounces to grams,	multiply by 28.35	10 oz. x 28.35	=	283.5 g.
meters (m) to feet,	multiply by 3.28	2 meters x 3.28	=	6.56 feet
feet to meters,	multiply by 0.3	6 feet x 0.3	=	1.8 meters

For fun, take your weight in pounds and convert it into kilograms. It sounds better that way, doesn't it? How many kilometers is it from your home to school, to work, to the post office?

The Simple Versions		
one liter	=	approximately one US quart
four liters	=	approximately one US gallon
one kilo	=	approximately 2.2 pounds
100 grams	=	approximately 3.5 ounces
500 grams	=	slightly more than one pound
one meter	=	slightly more than three feet

The distance between **New York y Madrid es** approximately 3,578 miles. How many kilometers would that be? It is 6,460 miles between **San Francisco y Buenos Aires.** How many kilometers is that?

kilometers (km.) to miles,	multiply by 0.62	1000 km. x 0.62	=	620 miles
miles to kilometers,	multiply by 1.6	1000 miles x 1.6	=	1,600 km.

Inches	1	2	3	4	5	6	7

To convert centimeters into inches, multiply by 0.39   Example: 9 cm. x 0.39   =   3.51 in.

To convert inches into centimeters, multiply by 2.54   Example: 4 in. x 2.54   =   10.16 cm.

cm 1	2	3	4	5	6	7	8	9	10	11	12	13	14	15	16	17	18

Sí, también hay *(ah-ee)* bills to pay **en México o en España. Usted** have just finished your delicious <small>there are</small>

dinner **y usted quiere** *(kee-eh-reh)* **pagar la cuenta. ¿Qué hace usted? Usted llama el camarero** *(kah-mah-reh-roh)* **o la** <small>want</small> *(ah-seh)* <small>do</small> <small>waiter</small>

camarera *(kah-mah-reh-rah)* (sometimes called **el mesero** *(meh-sair-oh)* **o la mesera** *(meh-sair-ah)*). **El mesero** will normally reel off what <small>waitress</small> <small>waiter</small> <small>waitress</small>

usted have eaten while writing rapidly. **Él** will then place a piece **de papel** on **la mesa y dice,**

"**Son trescientos pesos en total.**" *(toh-tahl)* **Usted** will pay **el mesero o** perhaps **usted** will pay **un**

cajero. *(kah-heh-roh)* <small>cashier</small>

Being a seasoned traveler, **usted** know that tipping as **nosotros** know it **en los Estados**

Unidos can vary from country to country. If the service is not included **en la cuenta,** round the

bill up **o** simply leave what you consider an appropriate amount for your **mesero sobre la mesa.**

When **usted** dine out on **su viaje,** *(soo)(vee-ah-heh)* it is always a good idea to make a reservation. It can be <small>your</small>

difficult to get into a popular **restaurante.** Nevertheless, the experience is well worth the

trouble **usted** might encounter to obtain a reservation. **Y** remember, **usted sabe** enough **español**

to make a reservation. Just speak slowly and clearly.

❐ **el silencio** *(see-len-see-oh)* . . . . silence		_____
❐ **simple** *(seem-pleh)* . . . . simple		_____
❐ **simultáneo** *(see-mool-tah-neh-oh)* . . . . simultaneous	**S**	_____
❐ **la sinfonía** *(seen-foh-nee-ah)* . . . . symphony		_____
❐ **el sistema** *(sees-teh-mah)* . . . . system		_____

Remember these key **palabras** when dining out, be it **en Perú o en Chile.**

(kah-mah-reh-roh) (meh-sair-oh)
el camarero/ mesero _____
waiter

(kah-mah-reh-rah) (meh-sair-ah)
la camarera/ mesera _____
waitress

(kwehn-tah)
la cuenta *la cuenta, la cuenta*
bill

(proh-pee-nah)
la propina _____
tip

(meh-noo)
el menú/la carta _____
menu

(kahm-bee-oh)
el cambio _____
change

(pair-doh-neh-meh)
perdóneme _____
excuse me

(grah-see-ahs)
gracias _____
thank you

(fah-vor)
por favor _____
please

(grah-tees)
gratis _____
free, no charge

(kohn-vair-sah-see-ohn)
Aquí está a sample **conversación** involving paying **la cuenta.**

Carlos: **Por favor, quiero pagar la cuenta.**
(fah-vor) *(kee-eh-roh)*
to pay

Por favor, quiero pagar la cuenta.

(heh-ren-teh)
Gerente: **¿El número del cuarto, por favor?**
manager
(kwar-toh)
room

_____

Carlos: **Cuarto trescientos diez.**

_____

Gerente: **Gracias. Un momento.**

_____

Gerente: **Aquí está la cuenta.**

_____

(kohn)
If **usted** have any problems **con números,** just ask someone to write out **los números,** so that

usted can be sure you understand everything correctly, **"Por favor, escriba usted los números."**
(es-kree-bah)
write out

Practice: _____
(Please write out the numbers. Thank you.)

❏ **social** *(soh-see-ahl)* .... social
❏ **el sofá** *(soh-fah)* .... sofa
❏ **sólido** *(soh-lee-doh)* .... solid
❏ **solitario** *(soh-lee-tah-ree-oh)* .... solitary
❏ **sudamericano** *(sood-ah-meh-ree-kah-noh)* ... South American

S

_____
_____
_____
_____
_____

Ahora, let's take a break from **las cuentas** *(kwehn-tahs)* **y el dinero** y learn some **nuevas** *(nweh-vahs)* fun **palabras.**

money · new

Usted can always practice these **palabras** by using your flash cards at the back of this **libro.**

Carry these flash cards in your purse, pocket, briefcase **o** knapsack **y** *use them!*

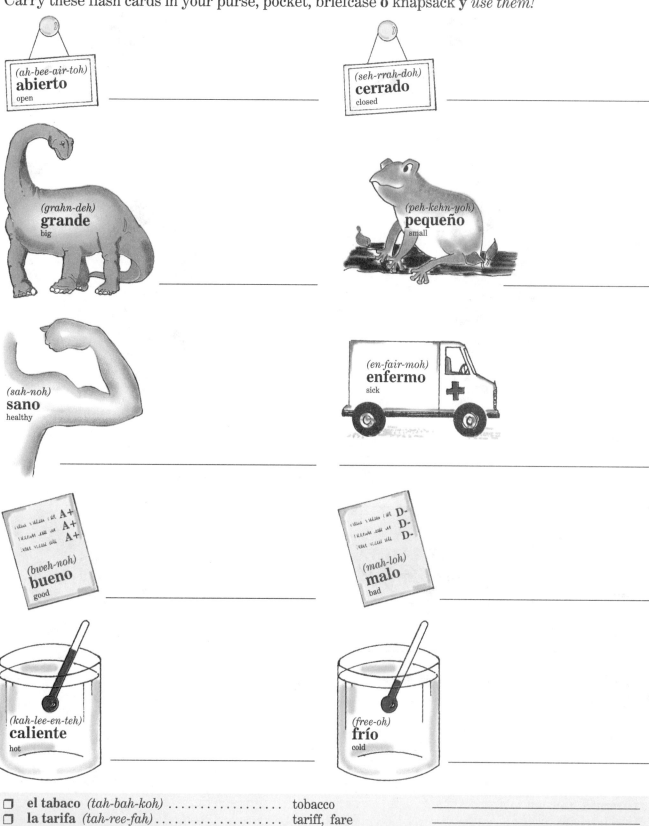

(ah-bee-air-toh)
abierto
open

(seh-rrah-doh)
cerrado
closed

(grahn-deh)
grande
big

(peh-kehn-yoh)
pequeño
small

(sah-noh)
sano
healthy

(en-fair-moh)
enfermo
sick

(bweh-noh)
bueno
good

(mah-loh)
malo
bad

(kah-lee-en-teh)
caliente
hot

(free-oh)
frío
cold

❑	**el tabaco** *(tah-bah-koh)*	tobacco	
❑	**la tarifa** *(tah-ree-fah)*	tariff, fare	
❑	**el taxi** *(tahk-see)*	taxi	**t**
❑	**el té** *(teh)*	tea	
❑	**el teatro** *(teh-ah-troh)*	theater	

(kor-toh)
corto _____
short

(lar-goh)
largo _____
long

(des-pah-see-oh)
despacio _____
slow

(rah-pee-doh)
rápido _____
fast

(ahl-toh)
alto _____
tall, high

(kor-toh)
corto _____
short

(vee-eh-hoh)
viejo _____
old

(hoh-ven)
joven _____
young

(kah-roh)
caro _____
expensive

(bah-rah-toh)
barato _____
inexpensive

(ree-koh)
rico _____
rich

(poh-breh)
pobre _____
poor

(moo-choh)
mucho _____
a lot

(poh-koh)
poco _____
a little

☐	**técnico** *(tek-nee-koh)*	technical	_____
☐	**el teléfono** *(teh-leh-foh-noh)*	telephone	_____
☐	**el telegrama** *(teh-leh-grah-mah)*	telegram	_____
☐	**la televisión** *(teh-leh-vee-see-ohn)*	television programming	_____
☐	**terminal** *(tair-mee-nahl)*	terminal	_____

t

Aquí están más verbos nuevos.

(sah-bair)
saber _____
to know (fact)

(poh-dair)
poder _____
to be able to, can

(leh-air)
leer _____
to read

(teh-nair) (keh)
tener que _____
to have to, must

Study the patterns **abajo** closely, as **usted** will use these verbs a lot.

Avenida
El Dorado

(sah-bair)
saber
to know

Yo _sé/_ _____ **todo.**
(toh-doh)
everything

Usted _____ **la dirección.**
(dee-rek-see-ohn)
address

Él _sabe/_ _____ **hablar el español.**
Ella
to speak

Nosotros _____ **el nombre del hotel.**
(oh-tel)
name

Ellos _____ **hablar el francés.**
Ellas

Me
llamo
Elena.

(poh-dair)
poder
to be able to, can

Yo _puedo/_ _____ **hablar el español.**
(ah-blar) *(es-pahn-yohl)*
to speak

Usted _puede/_ _____ **comprender el español.**
understand

Él _____ **leer el español.**
Ella
(leh-air)
read

Nosotros _podemos/_ _____ **hablar el inglés.**
(een-gles)

Ellos _pueden/_ _____ **entender el alemán.**
Ellas
(ah-leh-mahn)
German

(leh-air)
leer
to read

Yo _leo/_ _____ **el libro.**

Usted _____ **la revista.**
(reh-vees-tah)
magazine

Él _____ **el menú.**
Ella
(meh-noo)

Nosotros _leemos/_ _____ **mucho.**
a lot

Ellos _____ **el periódico.**
Ellas
(peh-ree-oh-dee-koh)
newspaper

(teh-nair) (keh)
tener que
to have to, must

Yo _tengo que/_ _____ **aprender el español.**
(ah-pren-dair)

Usted _____ **leer el libro.**
(leh-air)

Él _tiene que/_ _____ **comer ahora.**
Ella
(koh-mair)

Nosotros _____ **visitar Barcelona.**
(vee-see-tar)

Ellos _____ **pagar la cuenta.**
Ellas
(kwehn-tah)

☐ **la temperatura** *(tem-peh-rah-too-rah)*	temperature	_____
☐ **el termómetro** *(tair-moh-meh-troh)*	thermometer	_____
☐ **típico** *(tee-pee-koh)*	typical	**t** _____
☐ **el tomate** *(toh-mah-teh)*	tomato	_____
☐ **total** *(toh-tahl)*	total	_____

73

Notice that **"poder," "tener que," y "querer"** can be combined with another verb.

(kee-eh-roh)
Yo quiero pagar.
want

(koh-mair)
Yo quiero comer.
eat

(poh-deh-mohs)(leh-air)
Nosotros podemos leer el español.
can

Nosotros podemos pagar la cuenta.

(tee-en-eh)   (sah-leer)
Él tiene que salir.
must/has to   leave

Él tiene que pagar la cuenta.

(ah-pren-dair)
Quiero aprender el español.
I want

Puedo aprender el español.
I can

Tengo que aprender el español.
I must

(pweh-deh)
¿Puede usted translate the sentences **en español? Las respuestas están abajo.**
can

1. I can speak Spanish. _____

2. They can pay the bill. _____

3. He has to pay the bill. _____

4. We know the answer. _____ Nosotros sabemos la respuesta. _____

5. She knows a lot. _____

6. We can read Spanish. _____

7. I cannot find the hotel. _____

8. We are not able to (cannot) understand French. _____

9. I want to visit Madrid. _____

10. She reads the newspaper. _____

LAS RESPUESTAS

1. **Puedo hablar español.**
2. **Ellos pueden pagar la cuenta.**
3. **Él tiene que pagar la cuenta.**
4. **Nosotros sabemos la respuesta.**
5. **Ella sabe mucho.**

6. **Nosotros podemos leer el español.**
7. **Yo no puedo encontrar el hotel.**
8. **Nosotros no podemos comprender el francés.**
9. **Yo quiero visitar Madrid.**
10. **Ella lee el periódico.**

74

Ahora, draw **líneas** *(lee-neh-ahs)* **entre** *(en-treh)* the opposites **abajo.** **No** forget to say them out loud. Use
lines *between*

these **palabras** every day to describe **cosas en su** *(soo)* **casa, en su escuela** *(es-kweh-lah)* **y en su oficina.**
your home *school*

(grahn-deh)
grande

(ees-kee-air-dah)
izquierda

(hoh-ven)
joven

(poh-breh)
pobre

(sah-noh)
sano

(lar-goh)
largo

(moo-choh)
mucho

(bweh-noh)
bueno

(kah-lee-en-teh)
caliente

abajo

(des-pah-see-oh)
despacio

(kah-roh)
caro

(seh-rrah-doh)
cerrado

(ah-rree-bah)
arriba

(ah-bee-air-toh)
abierto

(kor-toh)
corto

(bah-rah-toh)
barato

(poh-koh)
poco

(en-fair-moh)
enfermo

(rah-pee-doh)
rápido

(vee-eh-hoh)
viejo

(peh-kehn-yoh)
pequeño

(deh-reh-chah)
derecha

(free-oh)
frío

(ree-koh)
rico

(mah-loh)
malo

Throughout **México usted puede encontrar** remarkable **y** *(mwee)* **muy viejas** ruins. **La vieja**
find

(pee-rah-mee-deh) *(sohl)*
Pirámide del Sol is less than 30 miles from Mexico City! Don't miss it! If **usted** travel **en**
sun

España, visit the many **(grandes y pequeños)** **castillos** *(kahs-tee-yohs)* **y palacios** *(pah-lah-see-ohs)* **magníficos.** *(mahg-nee-fee-kohs)*
castles *palaces*

☐ **trágico** *(trah-hee-koh)*	tragic	_____
☐ **tranquilo** *(trahn-kee-loh)*	tranquil, quiet	_____
☐ **transparente** *(trahns-pah-ren-teh)*	transparent	**t** _____
☐ **transportar** *(trahns-por-tar)*	to transport	_____
☐ **el tren** *(tren)*	train	_____

(vee-ah-har)
Viajar, Viajar, Viajar
to travel

(ah-yair) *(lee-mah)*
¡Ayer en Lima!
yesterday

(oy) *(kah-rah-kahs)*
¡Hoy en Caracas!
today

(sahn-tee-ah-goh)
¡Mañana en Santiago!
tomorrow

If you know a few key **palabras,** traveling can be easy in most Spanish-speaking countries. **El español** is spoken in over 20 countries around the world with each country adding its own character **y** flavor to the language. Keep in mind that Argentina alone would cover almost one-third of the European continent! ¿Cómo *(vee-ah-hah)* viaja usted?

(vee-ah-hah) *(kah-rroh)*
Pedro viaja en carro.
travels   car

(ah-vee-ohn)
Ana viaja por avión.
airplane

(moh-toh-see-kleh-tah)
Juan viaja en motocicleta.

Anita viaja por tren.

(bar-koh)
José viaja en barco.
boat

María viaja por autobús.

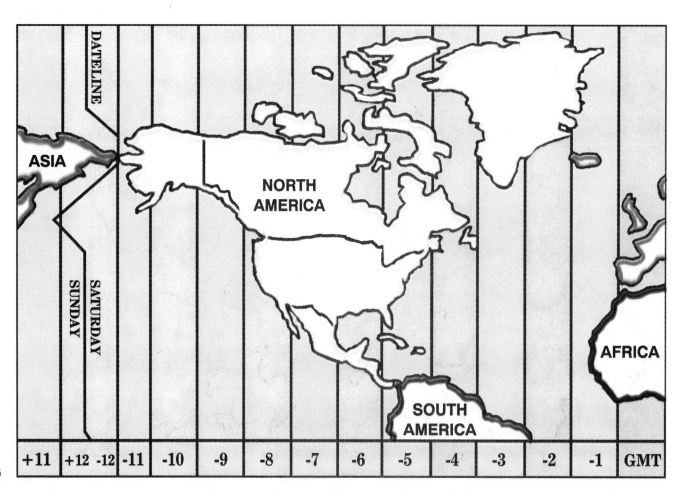

+11	+12	-12	-11	-10	-9	-8	-7	-6	-5	-4	-3	-2	-1	GMT

Cuándo usted are traveling, **usted** will want to tell others your nationality **y usted** will meet people from all corners of the world. Can you guess where someone is from if they say one of the following? **Las respuestas** are in your glossary beginning on page 108.

Yo soy de Inglaterra. _____
<small>am   from</small>

(ee-tah-lee-ah)
Soy de Italia. _____

(peh-roo)
Soy de Perú. _____

Soy de España. _____

(bel-hee-kah)
Soy de Bélgica. _____

(swee-sah)
Soy de Suiza. _____

Soy de Honduras. _____

Soy de Bolivia. _____

(ar-hen-tee-nah)
Soy de Argentina. _____

(frahn-see-ah)
Nosotros somos de Francia. _____

(ah-leh-mahn-ee-ah)
Somos de Alemania. _____

Somos de México. _____

Somos de Costa Rica. _____

(chee-leh)
Ella es de Chile. _____

(koo-bah)
Él es de Cuba. _____

(por-too-gahl)
Ella es de Portugal. _____

(ow-strah-lee-ah)
Él es de Australia. _____

(kah-nah-dah)
Yo soy de Canadá. _____

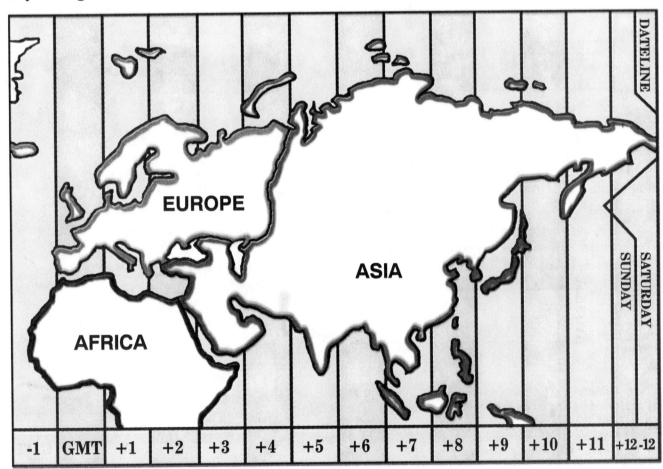

-1	GMT	+1	+2	+3	+4	+5	+6	+7	+8	+9	+10	+11	+12 -12

La palabra for "trip" is taken from **la palabra "viajar,"** which makes it easy: **viaje.** *(vee-ah-heh)* trip **Muchas palabras** revolve around the concept of travel, which is exactly what **usted quiere** to do. Practice the following **palabras** many times. **Usted** will see them often.

(vee-ah-har)
viajar _____
to travel

(vee-ah-heh-roh)
el viajero _____
traveler

(ah-hen-see-ah) *(vee-ah-hes)*
la agencia de viajes _____
travel agency

(bwehn)
¡Buen viaje! _____
have a good trip

If **usted** choose **viajar en coche,** *(koh-cheh)* **aquí están** a few key **palabras.**

(ow-toh-pees-tah) *(kah-rreh-tair-ah)*
la autopista/ carretera _____
freeway

(kah-mee-noh)
el camino _____
road

(kah-yeh)
la calle _____
street

(kah-rroh) *(ahl-kee-lair)*
el carro de alquiler _____
rental car

(ah-hen-see-ah) *(ahl-kee-lair)*
la agencia de carros de alquiler _____
car-rental agency

(es-tah-see-ohn) *(sair-vee-see-oh)*
la estación de servicio _____
service station

Abajo hay *(ah-ee)* there are some basic signs which **usted** should **también** learn to recognize quickly.

(en-trar)
entrar _____
to enter

(sah-leer)
salir _____
to exit

ENTRADA →

SALIDA →

(en-trah-dah)
la entrada _____
entrance

(sah-lee-dah)
la salida _____
exit

(preen-see-pahl)
la entrada principal _____
main

(oor-hen-see-ah)
la salida de urgencia _____
urgency (emergency)

EMPUJAR

TIRAR

(em-poo-har)
empujar _____
push (doors)

(tee-rar)
tirar _____
pull (doors)

❑ **el triángulo** *(tree-ahn-goo-loh)* . . . . triangle _____
❑ **triunfante** *(tree-oon-fahn-teh)* . . . . triumphant _____
❑ **trivial** *(tree-vee-ahl)* . . . . trivial _____
❑ **el trolebús** *(troh-leh-boos)* . . . . trolleybus _____
❑ **la trompeta** *(trohm-peh-tah)* . . . . trumpet _____

t

Let's learn the basic travel verbs. Take out a piece of paper **y** make up your own sentences with these **palabras nuevas.** Follow the same pattern **usted** have in previous Steps.

(voh-lar)
volar _____
to fly

(yeh-gar)
llegar _____
to arrive

(sah-leer)
salir _____
to leave

(ah-ee)
hay _____
there is, there are

(eer)   *(koh-cheh)*
ir en coche _____
to drive, to go by car

(par-teer)
partir _____
to depart (vehicles)

(ah-sair)   *(mah-leh-tah)*
hacer la maleta _____
to pack   suitcase

(kahm-bee-ar)
cambiar _____
to transfer (vehicles) or to change money!

(ah-ee)
Aquí hay some **palabras nuevas para el** *(vee-ah-heh)* **viaje.**
trip

(ah-eh-roh-pwair-toh)
el aeropuerto
airport

(ahn-den)
el andén
platform

(oh-rah-ree-oh)
el horario
timetable

DE MADRID A BARCELONA		
Partida	Nº de tren	Llegada
00:41	50	09:41
07:40	19	15:40
12:15	22	00:15
14:32	10	23:32
21:40	04	09:40

(es-tah-see-ohn)
la estación de tren
train station

☐ **tropical** *(troh-pee-kahl)* . . . . tropical _____
☐ **el tumulto** *(too-mool-toh)* . . . . tumult _____
☐ **el túnel** *(too-nel)* . . . . tunnel _____
☐ **el turista** *(too-rees-tah)* . . . . tourist _____
☐ **el tutor** *(too-tor)* . . . . tutor _____

t

Con estas palabras, usted está ready for any **viaje**, anywhere. **Usted** should have no problem *(es-tahs)* / these

con these verbs **nuevos**, just remember the basic "plug-in" formula **usted** have already

learned. Use that knowledge to translate the following thoughts **al español.** **Las respuestas** *(ahl)* / into

están abajo.

1. I fly to Buenos Aires. ⎯⎯⎯⎯⎯ *Yo vuelo a Buenos Aires.* ⎯⎯⎯⎯⎯

2. I change (transfer) in Bogotá. ⎯⎯⎯⎯⎯⎯⎯⎯⎯⎯⎯⎯⎯⎯⎯⎯⎯

3. He drives to Córdoba. ⎯⎯⎯⎯⎯⎯⎯⎯⎯⎯⎯⎯⎯⎯⎯⎯⎯⎯⎯⎯⎯

4. We leave tomorrow. ⎯⎯⎯⎯⎯⎯⎯⎯⎯⎯⎯⎯⎯⎯⎯⎯⎯⎯⎯⎯⎯⎯

5. We buy tickets to Málaga. ⎯⎯⎯⎯⎯⎯⎯⎯⎯⎯⎯⎯⎯⎯⎯⎯⎯⎯

6. They drive to Cabo San Lucas. ⎯⎯⎯⎯⎯⎯⎯⎯⎯⎯⎯⎯⎯⎯⎯⎯

7. Where is the train to Pamplona? ⎯⎯⎯⎯⎯⎯⎯⎯⎯⎯⎯⎯⎯⎯⎯

8. How can I fly to Spain? With American or with Iberia? ⎯⎯⎯⎯⎯⎯⎯⎯

Aquí hay some **palabras importantes para el viajero.**
(eem-por-tahn-tes) *(vee-ah-heh-roh)* / traveler

DE MADRID A MÁLAGA		
Partida	**Nº de tren**	**Llegada**
00:50	103	12:41
06:00	233	18:30
10:45	33	23:00
15:16	43	05:30
22:50	53	10:00

(oh-koo-pah-doh)
ocupado ⎯⎯⎯⎯⎯⎯⎯⎯⎯⎯⎯⎯
occupied

(par-tee-dah)
la partida ⎯⎯⎯⎯⎯⎯⎯⎯⎯⎯
departure

(lee-breh)
libre ⎯⎯⎯⎯⎯⎯⎯⎯⎯⎯⎯⎯⎯⎯
free

(yeh-gah-dah)
la llegada ⎯⎯⎯⎯⎯⎯⎯⎯⎯
arrival

(kohm-par-tee-mee-en-toh)
el compartimiento ⎯⎯⎯⎯⎯
compartment, wagon

(es-trahn-heh-roh)
extranjero ⎯⎯⎯⎯⎯⎯⎯⎯⎯
foreign

(ah-see-en-toh)
el asiento ⎯⎯⎯⎯⎯⎯⎯⎯⎯⎯
seat

(pah-ees)
del país ⎯⎯⎯⎯⎯⎯⎯⎯⎯⎯
domestic, internal (of the country)

Increase your travel **palabras** by writing out **las palabras abajo** y practicing the sample sentences out loud. Practice asking **preguntas con "dónde."** It will help you later.

(ah)
a _____
to   **¿Dónde está el tren a Madrid?**

(pwair-tah)
la puerta de entrada _____
gate   **¿Dónde está la puerta de entrada número ocho?**

(ohb-heh-tohs) (pair-dee-dohs)
la oficina de objetos perdidos _____
lost-and-found office   **¿Dónde está la oficina de objetos perdidos?**

(por-teh-roh)
el portero _____ ¿Donde está el portero? _____
porter   **¿Dónde está el portero?**

(vweh-loh)
el vuelo _____
flight   **¿Es éste el vuelo a Lima?**

(reh-klah-mah-see-ohn)   (mah-leh-tahs)
la reclamación de maletas _____
baggage claim   **¿Dónde está el reclamo de maletas?**

(kahm-bee-oh)
la oficina de cambio _____
money-exchange office   **¿Dónde hay una oficina de cambio?**

(tah-blair-oh)
el tablero _____
counter   **¿Dónde está el tablero número nueve?**

(sah-lah)   (es-pair-ah)
la sala de espera _____
waiting room   **¿Dónde está la sala de espera?**

(koh-cheh-koh-meh-dor)
el coche-comedor _____
dining car   **¿Hay un coche-comedor?**

(koh-cheh-kah-mah)
el coche-cama _____
sleeping car   **¿Dónde está el coche-cama número dos?**

(sek-see-ohn)   (foo-mar)
la sección de no fumar _____
non-smoking section   **¿Hay una sección de no fumar?**

_____ *(yeh-gah)*
¿ _____ **llega el tren?**
(when)   (when)

_____ *(pah-sah)*
¿ _____ **pasa?**
(what)   (what)   is happening

☐ **último** *(ool-tee-moh)*	ultimate, last	_____
☐ **el uniforme** *(oo-nee-for-meh)*	uniform	_____
☐ **la unión** *(oo-nee-ohn)*	union	**u** _____
☐ **la universidad** *(oo-nee-vair-see-dahd)*	university	_____
☐ **urbano** *(oor-bah-noh)*	urban	_____

¿Puede usted leer las *(frah-ses)* frases *(see-gee-en-tes)* siguientes?
can · read · phrases · following

← **Ahora usted está *(sen-tah-doh)* sentado en el avión y**
seated

usted *(vweh-lah)* vuela a España. Usted tiene el
fly

dinero, los billetes, el *(pah-sah-por-teh)* pasaporte, y las

maletas. *(mah-leh-tahs)* Ahora usted es *(too-rees-tah)* turista. Usted
suitcases · tourist

llega *(yeh-gah)* mañana a las 8:00. ¡Buen *(bwehn)* viaje!

¡Buena *(bweh-nah)* suerte *(swair-teh)*!

En España y en América Latina there are many different types of trains – **el tren correo *(koh-rreh-oh)* es**
mail (local)

muy *(des-pah-see-oh)* despacio; el tren *(ek-spreh-soh)* expresso y el tren rápido are much faster. If **usted** plan to travel a long

distance, **usted** may wish to catch an Inter-City **tren o un tren *(ek-spreh-soh)* expresso de largo *(reh-koh-rree-doh)* recorrido**
distance

which would travel faster **y** make fewer intermediate stops.

❒	**urgente** *(oor-hen-teh)*	urgent		
❒	**usar** *(oo-sar)*	to use		
❒	**usual** *(oo-soo-ahl)*	usual	**u**	
❒	**el utensilio** *(oo-ten-see-lee-oh)*	utensil		
❒	**la utilidad** *(oo-tee-lee-dahd)*	utility		

Knowing these travel **palabras** will make your holiday twice as enjoyable **y** at least three times as easy. Drill yourself on this Step by selecting other destinations **y** ask your own **preguntas** about **trenes, autobuses, o aviones** that go there. Select **las palabras nuevas de** your **diccionario** *(deek-see-oh-nar-ee-oh)* **y** ask your own questions beginning with **cuándo**, **dónde**, **y** **cuánto cuesta**. **Las respuestas** to the crossword puzzle are at the bottom of the next page.

ACROSS

1. to buy
3. what
5. twenty
6. a (♂)
7. to know
9. restaurant
14. pencil
15. sick
16. it is
17. monetary unit of **México**
19. excuse me
23. children (♂ or mixed)
24. to say
26. bad
28. one hundred
30. to travel
32. well
36. to speak
38. give me
39. she

DOWN

1. bill
2. (I) need
3. (I) want
8. ladies (restroom)
10. time, weather
11. cold
12. to do, to make
14. (I) read
17. tip
18. to leave, to depart
20. to write
22. station
23. nothing
25. computer
26. suitcase
27. to drink
29. number
30. to live
31. to repeat
33. to enter
37. railway platform

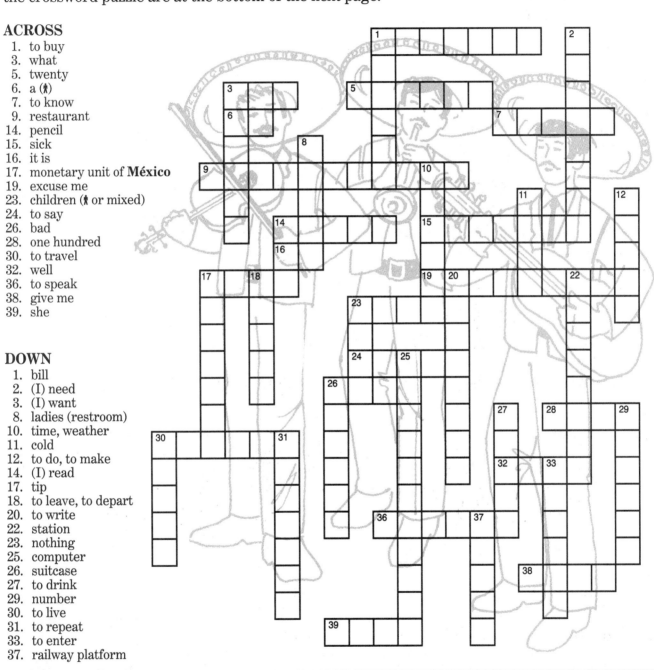

Mariachis – street musicians traditionally clad in black suits, a custom dating back to the 18th century. A group of mariachis usually includes a guitarist, violinist and a trumpeter.

What about inquiring about the price of **billetes?** *(bee-yeh-tes)* **Usted puede** ask these **preguntas.** *(preh-goon-tahs)*

tickets / can

¿Cuánto cuesta un billete a Sevilla? *(seh-vee-yah)* _____

¿Cuánto cuesta un billete a Barcelona? _____

¿Cuánto cuesta un billete a Lisboa? *(lees-boh-ah)* _____

boleto sencilla *(boh-leh-toh) (sen-see-yah)* _____
one-way ticket

ida y vuelta *(vwel-tah)* _____
round trip

What about times of **salida y llegado?** *(yeh-gah-doh)* **¡Usted puede preguntar eso también!**

departure / arrival / ask

¿Cuándo sale el avión para Valencia? *(sah-leh)* _____
when / departs / for

¿Cuándo sale el avión para Londres? _____

¿Cuándo llega el avión de Santiago? *(yeh-gah)* _____
arrives / from

¿Cuándo llega el avión de Cartagena? _____

¿Cuándo sale el avión para Panama? _____

Usted have just arrived **en España. Usted está en la estación de tren. ¿Dónde quiere usted ir? ¿a Córdoba? ¿a Barcelona?** Tell that to the person at **la ventanilla** selling **billetes!** *(ven-tah-nee-yah)*
window

Quiero ir a Granada. *(eer) (grah-nah-dah)* _____
go

¿Cuándo sale el tren para Granada? *(sah-leh)* _____

¿Cuánto cuesta un billete a Granada? _____

LAS RESPUESTAS

ACROSS		DOWN	
1. comprar	16. es	1. cuenta	14. leo
3. qué	17. peso	2. necesito	12. hacer
5. veinte	19. perdóneme	3. quiero	11. frío
6. un	23. niños	8. damas	10. tiempo
7. saber	24. decir	36. hablar	22. estación
9. restaurante	26. malo	38. dame	20. escribir
14. lápiz	28. cien	39. ella	23. nada
15. enfermo	30. viajar	32. bien	25. computadora
		17. propina	26. maleta
		18. salir	27. beber
		29. número	37. andén
		30. vivir	33. entrar
		31. repetir	

84

Ahora that **usted** know the words essential for traveling – be it throughout **España, México, Perú o Argentina** – what are some speciality items **usted** might go in search of?

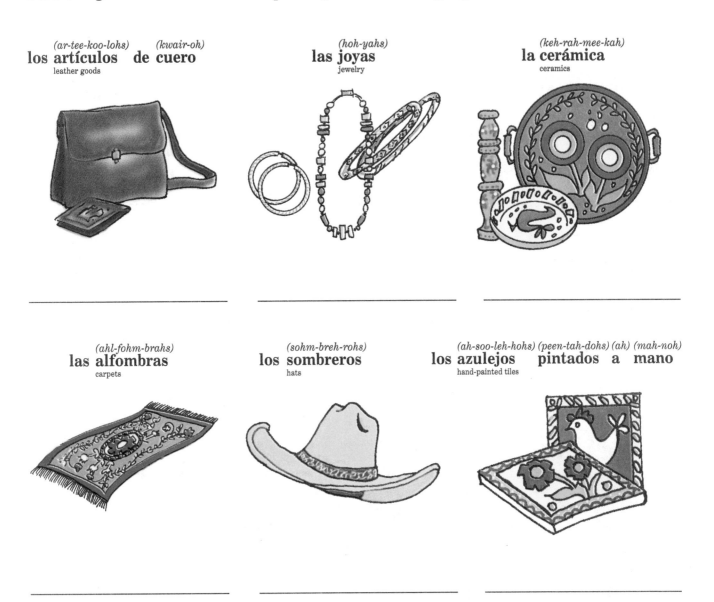

(ar-tee-koo-lohs) *(kwair-oh)*
los artículos de cuero
leather goods

(hoh-yahs)
las joyas
jewelry

(keh-rah-mee-kah)
la cerámica
ceramics

(ahl-fohm-brahs)
las alfombras
carpets

(sohm-breh-rohs)
los sombreros
hats

(ah-soo-leh-hohs) (peen-tah-dohs) (ah) (mah-noh)
los azulejos pintados a mano
hand-painted tiles

Consider using SPANISH *a language map*® as well. SPANISH *a language map*® is the perfect companion for your travels when **usted** may not wish to take along this **libro**. Each section focuses on essentials for your **viaje**. Your *Language Map*® is not meant to replace learning **español**, but will help you in the event **usted** forget something and need a little bit of help. For more information about the *Language Map*® Series, please turn to page 132.

For more information about the *Language Map*® Series, please turn to page 132.

☐ **el valle** *(vah-yeh)*	valley	_____
☐ **la vanidad** *(vah-nee-dahd)*	vanity	_____
☐ **varios** *(vah-ree-ohs)*	various **v**	_____
☐ **el vaso** *(vah-soh)*	glass (of water)	_____
☐ **el Vaticano** *(vah-tee-kah-noh)*	the Vatican	_____

20

La Carta o El Menú
(kar-tah) *(meh-noo)*

menu

Usted está ahora en Venezuela o Colombia y usted tiene un cuarto en un hotel. Usted

tiene hambre. *(ahm-breh)* ¿Dónde hay un restaurante bueno? First of all, **hay** different types of places

hunger   is there

to eat. Let's learn them.

el restaurante *(res-tow-rahn-teh)*

exactly what it says with a variety of meals

el café *(kah-feh)*

a coffee house **con** snacks **y** beverages

la fonda/el parador *(fohn-dah) (pah-rah-dor)*

an inn with a full range of meals. In **España** especially, several places of historic interest have

been preserved and converted into **paradores**, so **usted** often get history, scenery and good food!

la cantina/ la taberna *(kahn-tee-nah) (tah-bair-nah)*

a bar – but wait! Many bars in **España** have a large variety of hot and cold snacks called **tapas** *(tah-pahs)*

which can be combined for an interesting and flavorful meal.

If **usted** look around you **en un restaurante, usted** will see that some **costumbres hispanas** *(kohs-toom-bres) (ees-pah-nahs)*

customs

might be different from yours. Sharing **mesas con** others **es** a common **y muy** pleasant custom.

Before beginning your **comida,** *(koh-mee-dah)* be sure to wish those sharing your table – "**¡Que aproveche!**" *(keh) (ah-proh-veh-cheh)*

meal   enjoy your meal

Your turn to practice now.

_____
(enjoy your meal)

And at least one more time for practice!

_____
(enjoy your meal)

☐ **el vehículo** *(veh-hee-koo-loh)* .... vehicle			_____
☐ **el vinagre** *(vee-nah-greh)*.................. vinegar			_____
☐ **el vino** *(vee-noh)* .... wine	**v**		_____
☐ **el violín** *(vee-oh-leen)* .... violin			_____
☐ **la visa** *(vee-sah)*..................... visa			

Start imagining now all the new taste treats you will experience abroad. Try all of the different types of eating establishments mentioned on the previous page. Experiment. If **usted**

(en-kwehn-trah)
encuentra un restaurante that **usted** would like to try, consider calling ahead to make a

(reh-sair-vah-see-ohn)
reservación:

(kee-see-eh-rah)
"**Yo quisiera una reservación.**"
I   would like

_____

(I would like a reservation.)

If **usted necesita una carta**, catch the

attention of **el mesero**, saying,

(pair-dohn)
"**Perdón. ¡La carta, por favor!**"
excuse me

_____

(Excuse me. Please, the menu!)

If your **mesero** asks if **usted** enjoyed your

comida, a smile **y** a "**Sí, muchas gracias,**" will

tell him that you did.

Most **restaurantes españoles** post **la carta** outside **o** inside. Do not hesitate to ask to see **la**

carta before being seated so **usted sabe** what type of **comidas y precios usted** will encounter.
                                                                                    meals   prices

(koo-bee-air-toh)
Most **restaurantes** offer **un cubierto.** This is a complete **comida** at a fair **precio.** Always
                            special meal of the day   meal   price

look for the **plato del día** as well.
              dish

☐	**la visita** *(vee-see-tah)*	visit			_____
☐	**visitar** *(vee-see-tar)*	to visit	**V**		_____
☐	**el zodíaco** *(soh-dee-ah-koh)*	zodiac			_____
☐	**la zona** *(soh-nah)*	zone	**Z**		_____
☐	**la zoología** *(soh-oh-loh-hee-ah)*	zoology			_____

En España, México y los **países** *(pah-ees-es)* sudamericanos y centroamericanos, **hay** **tres** main meals
_{countries} _{there are}

to enjoy every day, plus perhaps pastry **por** the tired traveler in **la tarde**.
_{for} _{afternoon}

el desayuno *(deh-sah-yoo-noh)* _____
_{breakfast}

en hoteles y pensiones, this meal usually consists of coffee, tea, rolls, butter and marmalade.
Check serving times before **usted** retire for the night or you might miss out!

el almuerzo *(ahl-mwair-soh)* _____
_{mid-day meal}

generally served from 12:00 to 15:00, followed by a **siesta** or period of quiet. Shops close down
to reopen around 15:00 or 16:00.

la comida/ cena *(koh-mee-dah) (sehn-ah)* _____
_{evening meal}

generally served from 20:00 to midnight

Ahora for a preview of delights to come . . . At the back of this **libro, usted** will find a sample

carta española. **Lea usted la carta hoy y aprenda usted las palabras nuevas.** When **usted**
_{read} *(leh-ah)* _{today} _{learn}

are ready to leave on your **viaje,** cut out **la carta,** fold it, **y** carry it in your pocket, wallet **o**

purse. Before you go, how do **usted** say these **tres** phrases which are so very important for the

hungry traveler?

Excuse me. I would like a reservation. _____

Waiter! Please, give me a menu. _____

Enjoy your meal! _____

¿ _____ **come la ensalada?**   ¿ _____ **bebe té?**
_(who) _{eats}   _(who) _{drinks}

¿ _____ **viaja a Honduras?**
_(who)

(who)

Learning the following should help you to identify what kind of meat **usted** have ordered **y cómo** it will be prepared.
☐ **vaca** *(vah-kah)* . . . . beef   _____
☐ **ternera** *(tair-neh-rah)* . . . . veal   _____
☐ **cerdo** *(sair-doh)* . . . . pork   _____
☐ **carnero** *(kar-neh-roh)* . . . . mutton

El menú below has the main categories usted will find in most restaurants. Learn them hoy so that usted will easily recognize them when you dine en Madrid, Bogotá o Lima. Be sure to write the words in the blanks below.

(meh-noo)
Menú

(en-treh-meh-ses)
entremeses
appetizers

(soh-pahs)
sopas
soup

(hoo-eh-vohs)
huevos
eggs

(pes-cah-doh)
pescado
fish dishes

(kar-neh)
carne
meat dishes

(ah-vehs) *(kah-sah)*
aves y caza
poultry and game

(leh-goom-bres)
legumbres
vegetables

(en-sah-lah-dahs)
ensaladas
salad

(pohs-tres)
postres
dessert

(boh-kah-dee-yohs)
bocadillos
sandwiches

(froo-tah) *(keh-soh)*
fruta o queso
fruit cheese

(pahs-teh-les)
pasteles
pastries

(beh-bee-dahs)
bebidas
beverages

☐ **ave** *(ah-veh)* . . . . poultry
☐ **cordero** *(kor-deh-roh)* . . . . lamb
☐ **caza** *(kah-sah)* . . . . game
☐ **frito** *(free-toh)* . . . . fried
☐ **asado** *(ah-sah-doh)* . . . . roasted

Usted **también** *(tahm-bee-en)* will get **legumbres con** your **comida, y** perhaps **una ensalada mixta.** **Un día**
(tahm-bee-en) also *(leh-goom-bres)* vegetables meal *(mees-tah)* mixed

at an open-air **mercado** will teach you **los nombres** for all the different kinds of **legumbres y**
(mair-kah-doh) *(nohm-bres)*

frutas, plus it will be a delightful experience for you. **Usted puede** always consult your menu
(froo-tahs) fruit

guide at the back of this **libro** if **usted** forget **los nombres correctos.** **Ahora usted** are seated **y**

el camarero arrives.
waiter

¡La carta, por favor!

¿Y para beber?

Un vaso de vino blanco, por favor.

El desayuno **es un poco diferente** because **es** fairly standardized **y usted** will frequently take
(deh-sah-yoo-noh) breakfast it is

it at your **pensión,** as **está incluido** **en el precio del cuarto. Abajo** is a sample of what
(pehn-see-ohn) guest house/hotel *(een-kloo-ee-doh)* included price room

usted puede expect to greet you **por la mañana.**

Bebidas		**y . . .**
café		**queso**
		cheese
té		**croissant**
chocolate		**pan y panecillos**
		bread rolls
jugo de naranja		**mermelada**
juice orange		jam
jugo de tomate		**mantequilla**
jugo de toronja		**huevo pasado por agua**
grapefruit		soft-boiled
jugo de manzana		**tortillas** *(tor-tee-yahs)*
		omelettes
leche		

▢ **cocido** *(koh-see-doh)* . . . . cooked _____
▢ **al horno** *(ahl)(or-noh)* . . . . baked _____
▢ **a la parrilla** *(ah)(lah)(pah-rree-yah)* . . . . grilled _____
▢ **a la Romana** *((ah)(lah)(roh-mah-nah)* . . . . in batter _____
▢ **cocido al vapor** *(koh-see-doh)(ahl)(vah-por)* . . . . steamed _____

Aquí está an example of what **usted** might select for your evening meal. Using your menu guide on pages 117 and 118, as well as what **usted** have learned in this Step, fill in the blanks *in English* with what **usted** believe your **camarero** will bring you. **Las respuestas están** below.
answers

Entremés
Coctel de mariscos al estilo tradicional de España

_____

Ensaladas
Ensalada del tiempo con pan francés fresco

_____

Plato Principal
Trucha a la parrilla con mantequilla de limón y eneldo

_____

Postre
Manzanas rellenas con helado hecho en casa

_____

(when) (how) (why)

Ahora es a good time for a quick review. Draw lines between **las palabras españolas y** their English equivalents.

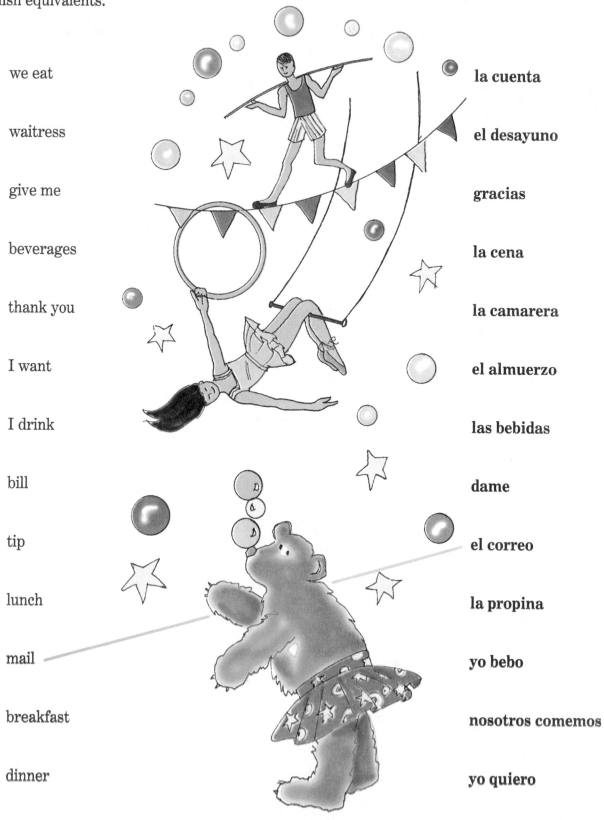

we eat

waitress

give me

beverages

thank you

I want

I drink

bill

tip

lunch

mail

breakfast

dinner

la cuenta

el desayuno

gracias

la cena

la camarera

el almuerzo

las bebidas

dame

el correo

la propina

yo bebo

nosotros comemos

yo quiero

Aquí are a few holidays which you might experience during your visit.

☐ **Año Viejo** *(ahn-yoh)(vee-eh-hoh)* . . . . New Year's Eve
☐ **Año Nuevo** *(ahn-yoh)(nweh-voh)* . . . . New Year's Day
☐ **Pascua** *(pahs-kwah)* . . . . Easter
92 ☐ **Viernes Santo** *(vee-air-nes)(sahn-toh)* . . . . Good Friday

21

El Teléfono
(teh-leh-foh-noh)
telephone

What is different about **el teléfono** *(teh-leh-foh-noh)* **en México o España?** Well, **usted** never notice such things until **usted quiere** to use them. **Los teléfonos** allow you to call **amigos,** *(ah-mee-gohs)* friends reserve **billetes** *(bee-yeh-tes)* tickets **de teatro, de ballet, o de concierto,** make calls **de urgencia,** check on the hours of **un museo,** rent **un carro, y** all those other things which **nosotros hacemos** *(ah-seh-mohs)* do on a daily basis. It **también** gives you a certain amount of freedom when **usted puede hacer** *(ah-sair)* make your own calls.

Having **un teléfono en su casa no es** *(soo)* your as common in some areas as **en los Estados Unidos.** That means that **usted puede encontrar cabinas** *(kah-bee-nahs)* find booths **de teléfono** – **teléfonos públicos** *(poo-blee-kohs)* public – everywhere.

So, let's learn how to operate **el teléfono.**

Las instrucciones can look instructions **complicadas,** *(kohm-plee-kah-dahs)* complicated but remember, some of these **palabras usted** should be able to recognize already. Ready? Well, before you turn the page it would be a good idea to go back **y** review all your numbers one more time.

To dial from the United States to most other countires **usted** need that country's international area code. Your **guía telefónica** *(gee-ah) (teh-leh-foh-nee-kah)* telephone book at home should have a listing of international area codes.

Aquí are some **muy** useful words built around the word, "**teléfono.**"
- ☐ **la operadora** *(oh-pair-ah-dor-ah)* .... operator
- ☐ **la cabina de teléfono** *(kah-bee-nah)(deh)(teh-leh-foh-noh)* .. public telephone booth
- ☐ **la guía telefónica** *(gee-ah)(teh-leh-foh-nee-kah)* ...... telephone book
- ☐ **la conversación telefónica** *(kohn-vair-sah-see-ohn)* ..... telephone conversation

When **usted** leave your contact numbers with friends, family **o** business colleagues, **usted** should include your destination country's area code **y** city code whenever possible . For example,

Country Codes		City Codes	
Mexico	52	Mexico City	5
Spain	34	Madrid	1
		Barcelona	3
Colombia	57	Bogotá	1
Venezuela	58	Caracas	2
Chile	56	Santiago	2

To call from one city to another city while abroad, **usted** may need to go to **la oficina de correos**

o call **la operadora** *(oh-pair-ah-dor-ah)* in your hotel. Tell **la operadora, "Yo quiero llamar a los Estados Unidos,"**
operator

o "Quiero llamar a Canadá."

Now you try it: _____
(I want to call to the U.S.A.)

When answering **el teléfono,** pick up the receiver **y** say, **"Bueno,"** o "_____".
(your name)

Someone answering **el teléfono** may simply say, "**Diga**" *(dee-gah)* **o "¿Con quién?**" *(kee-en)* which is short for
speak / with whom

"**¿Con quién hablo yo?**" *(ah-bloh)* Don't let it fluster you.
with whom am I speaking

When saying goodbye, say "**Hasta luego,**" *(ahs-tah) (lweh-goh)* or "**Hasta mañana,**" *(ahs-tah) (mahn-yah-nah)* or simply "**Adiós.**" *(ah-dee-ohs)*
until then / until tomorrow / goodbye

Your turn —

_____
(Hello. This is . . .)

_____   _____
(goodbye)   (until tomorrow)

Do not forget that **usted puede preguntar** . . . *(preh-goon-tar)*
can ask

¿Cuánto cuesta una llamada a los Estados Unidos? _____
U.S.A.

¿Cuánto cuesta una llamada a Inglaterra? *(een-glah-teh-rrah)* _____
England

Aquí are free telephone calls.
- ☐ **policía** *(poh-lee-see-ah)* . . . . police 101 _____
- ☐ **incendio** *(een-sen-dee-oh)* . . . . fire 102 _____
- ☐ **médico** *(meh-dee-koh)* . . . . doctor 103 _____
- ☐ **información** *(een-for-mah-see-ohn)* . . . . information 104 _____

Aquí **hay** *(ah-ee)* some sample telephone phrases. Write them in the blanks **abajo.**

Yo quiero *(kee-eh-roh)* **llamar** *(yah-mar)* **a Detroit.** _____
call

Yo quiero llamar a la Aerolínea Mexicana en la Ciudad de México. _____

Yo quiero llamar a un *(oon)* **médico.** *(meh-dee-koh)* _____
doctor

Mi *(mee)* **número** *(noo-meh-roh)* **es el 34-29-74.** _____
my

¿Cuál *(kwahl)* **es su** *(soo)* **número?** _____
what   your

¿Cuál es el número del *(oh-tel)* **hotel?** _____
of the

María: **Buenos días. Aquí María Mendoza. Quiero hablar con el Señor Galdés.**
to speak

_____

Secretaria: **Un momento. Lo siento.** *(see-en-toh)* **Su teléfono está ocupado.** *(oh-koo-pah-doh)*
one   I am sorry   his   busy

_____

María: **Repita** *(reh-pee-tah)* **usted eso** *(eh-soh)* **por favor.**
repeat   this

_____

Secretaria: **Lo siento. El teléfono está ocupado.**

_____

María: **Ah. Muchas gracias. Adiós.**

_____

Ahora usted are ready to use any **teléfono,** anywhere. Just take it slowly **y** speak clearly.

Here are countries where **español** is spoken that **usted** may wish to call.
☐ **Argentina** *(ar-hen-tee-nah)* . . . . Argentina   _____
☐ **Bolivia** *(boh-lee-vee-ah)* . . . . Bolivia   _____
☐ **Chile** *(chee-leh)* . . . . Chile   _____
☐ **Colombia** *(koh-lohm-bee-ah)* . . . . Columbia   _____

22

El *(meh-troh)* Metro
subway

"El metro" *(meh-troh)* es el nombre español para "the subway." In many cities, **el metro** is an extensive

system with express lines to the suburbs. **El tranvía** *(trahn-vee-ah)* is also a good means of transportation,
streetcar

plus **usted puede** see your surroundings on **el tranvía**. *(trahn-vee-ah)*

el metro *(meh-troh)*
subway

el tranvía *(trahn-vee-ah)*
streetcar

la parada *(pah-rah-dah)* **de metro**
stop

la parada de tranvía
stop

la parada de autobús *(ow-toh-boos)*
stop

Maps displaying the various **líneas** *(lee-nee-ahs)* **y** **paradas** *(pah-rah-dahs)* are generally posted outside every
lines   stops

entrada *(en-trah-dah)* **al metro.** *(ahl)* Almost every **kiosco** *(kee-ohs-koh)* **y** **agencia** *(ah-hen-see-ah)* **de viajes** has **un horario.** *(oh-rah-ree-oh)* **Las**
entrance   to the   newsstand   travel agency   schedule

líneas *(lee-nee-ahs)* are generally color-coded to facilitate reading just like your example on the next page.

How do **usted** use **el metro?** Check **el nombre** of the last **parada** on **la línea** which **usted**

want to take **y** catch **el metro** traveling in that direction. The same applies for **el tranvía**.

❏ **Costa Rica** *(kohs-tah)(ree-kah)*	Costa Rica
❏ **Cuba** *(koo-bah)*	Cuba
❏ **Ecuador** *(eh-kwah-dor)*	Ecuador
❏ **España** *(es-pahn-yah)*	Spain
❏ **Guatemala** *(gwah-tah-mah-lah)*	Guatemala

Ahora, locate your destination, select the **correct line** on your practice **metro y** hop on board.

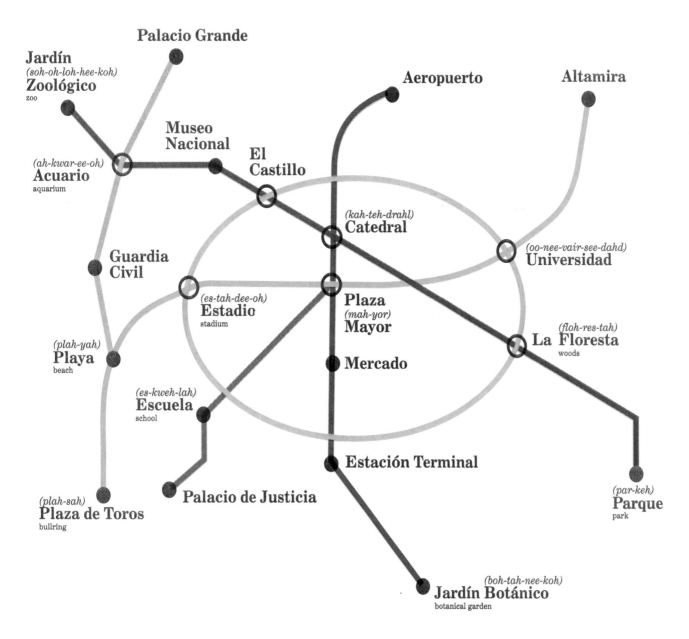

Palacio Grande

Jardín
(soh-oh-loh-hee-koh)
Zoológico
zoo

Aeropuerto

Altamira

Museo
Nacional

El
Castillo

(ah-kwar-ee-oh)
Acuario
aquarium

(kah-teh-drahl)
Catedral

(oo-nee-vair-see-dahd)
Universidad

Guardia
Civil

(es-tah-dee-oh)
Estadio
stadium

Plaza
(mah-yor)
Mayor

(floh-res-tah)
La Floresta
woods

(plah-yah)
Playa
beach

Mercado

(es-kweh-lah)
Escuela
school

Estación Terminal

(plah-sah)
Plaza de Toros
bullring

Palacio de Justicia

(par-keh)
Parque
park

(boh-tah-nee-koh)
Jardín Botánico
botanical garden

Say these questions aloud many times and don't forget your tokens **o** your card for **el metro.**

(pah-rah-dah)
¿Dónde está la parada de metro?

¿Dónde está la parada de autobús?

¿Dónde está la parada de tranvía?

METRO

☐ **México** *(meh-hee-koh)* . . . . Mexico
☐ **Panamá** *(pah-nah-mah)* . . . . Panama
☐ **Paraguay** *(pah-rah-gwhy)* . . . . Paraguay
☐ **Perú** *(peh-roo)* . . . . Peru
☐ **Venezuela** *(ven-es-weh-lah)* . . . . Venezuela

Practice the following basic **preguntas** *(preh-goon-tahs)* out loud **y** then write them in the blanks below.
questions

1. ¿Cada cuánto **viene** *(vee-en-eh)* el metro? _____
    how often *comes*

    ¿Cada cuánto viene el tranvía? _____

    ¿Cada cuánto viene el autobús? _____

2. ¿Cuándo *(kwahn-doh)* viene el metro? _____

    ¿Cuándo viene el tranvía? _____ *¿Cúando viene el tranvía?* _____

    ¿Cuándo viene el autobús? _____

3. ¿Cuánto *(kwahn-toh)* cuesta *(kwes-tah)* un billete para el metro? _____

    ¿Cuánto cuesta un billete para el tranvía? _____

    ¿Cuánto cuesta un billete para el autobús? _____

4. ¿Dónde **puedo** *(pweh-doh)* comprar un billete para el metro? _____
    can (I) *buy*

    ¿Dónde puedo comprar un billete para el tranvía? _____

    ¿Dónde puedo comprar un billete para el autobús? _____

Let's change directions **y** learn **tres** new verbs. **Usted** know the basic "plug-in" formula, so

write out your own sentences using these new verbs.

(lah-var)
lavar   _____
to wash

(pair-dair)
perder   _____
to lose

(doo-rar)
durar   _____
to last

Aquí are a few more holidays to keep in mind.
- ☐ **Día del Trabajo** *(dee-ah)(del)(trah-bah-hoh)* . . . . Labor Day
- ☐ **Nochebuena** *(noh-cheh-bweh-nah)* . . . . Christmas Eve
- ☐ **Navidad** *(nah-vee-dahd)* . . . . Christmas
- ☐ **Todos los Santos** *(toh-dohs)(lohs)(sahn-tohs)* . . . . All Saint's Day

23

Vender y Comprar
(ven-dair) *(kohm-prar)*
to sell   to buy

Shopping abroad is exciting. The simple everyday task of buying **un litro de leche o una**
(lee-troh) *(leh-cheh)*
liter   milk

(mahn-zah-nah)
manzana becomes a challenge that **usted** should **ahora** be able to meet quickly **y** easily. Of
apple

course, **usted** will purchase **recuerdos, sellos y tarjetas postales** but do not forget those many
(reh-kwair-dohs)
souvenirs

other items ranging from shoelaces to aspirin that **usted** might need unexpectedly. Locate your

store, draw a line to it **y,** as always, write your new words in the blanks provided.

(ahl-mah-sen)
el almacén _____
department store

(see-neh)
el cine _____
cinema

(koh-rreh-ohs)
la oficina de correos _____
post office

(bahn-koh)
el banco _____
bank

(oh-tel)
el hotel _____
hotel, inn

(es-tah-see-ohn) *(sair-vee-see-oh)*
la estación de servicio _____
service station

(kar-nee-seh-ree-ah)
la carnicería
butcher shop

(lee-breh-ree-ah)
la librería
bookstore

Las tiendas are generally **abiertas** *(ah-bee-air-tahs)* from
open
8:00 or 8:30 until 19:00. Keep in mind, many

shops close over the lunch hour.

_____   _____

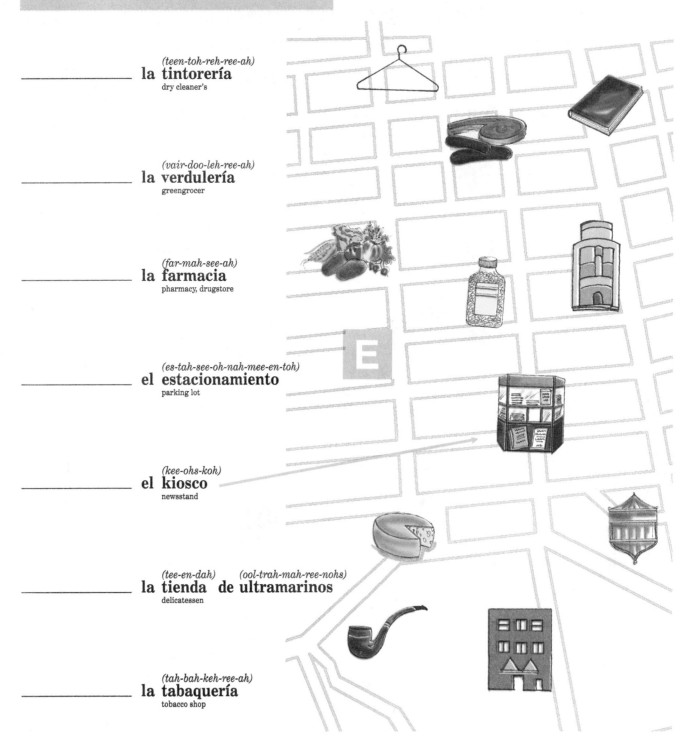

(teen-toh-reh-ree-ah)
_____ **la tintorería**
dry cleaner's

(vair-doo-leh-ree-ah)
_____ **la verdulería**
greengrocer

(far-mah-see-ah)
_____ **la farmacia**
pharmacy, drugstore

(es-tah-see-oh-nah-mee-en-toh)
_____ **el estacionamiento**
parking lot

(kee-ohs-koh)
_____ **el kiosco**
newsstand

(tee-en-dah)   *(ool-trah-mah-ree-nohs)*
_____ **la tienda de ultramarinos**
delicatessen

(tah-bah-keh-ree-ah)
_____ **la tabaquería**
tobacco shop

Los sábados, las tiendas están abiertas por
in
la **mañana**, but not always **por la tarde**.

¡Los domingos, las tiendas están **cerradas**! *(seh-rrah-dahs)*
closed

(ah-hen-see-ah)   *(vee-ah-hes)*
la agencia de viajes
travel agency

(poh-lee-see-ah)
la policía
police

_____   _____

100

(leh-cheh-ree-ah)
la lechería
dairy

_____

(floh-reh-ree-ah)
la florería
florist

_____

(pehs-kah-deh-ree-ah)
la pescadería _____
fish store

(tee-en-dah) *(kah-mah-rahs)*
la tienda de cámaras _____
camera supplies

(mair-kah-doh)
el mercado _____
market

(koh-mes-tee-bles)
la tienda de comestibles _____
food store

(reh-loh-heh-ree-ah)
la relojería _____
watchmaker's shop

(pah-nah-deh-ree-ah)
la panadería _____ la panadería _____
bakery

(pahs-teh-leh-ree-ah)
la pastelería _____
pastry shop

(lah-vahn-deh-ree-ah)
la lavandería _____
laundry

Everywhere but **en los Estados Unidos**, the
ground floor is called exactly that - **la**
(plahn-tah) *(bah-hah)*   *(pree-mair)* *(pee-soh)*
planta baja (PB). The **primer piso es**
                                        first floor
the next floor up **y** so on.

(pah-peh-leh-ree-ah)
la papelería
stationery store

_____

(peh-loo-keh-ree-ah)
la peluquería
hairdresser

_____

101

24

El Almacén
(ahl-mah-sen)
department store

At this point, **usted** should just about be ready for your **viaje.** **Usted** have gone shopping for

those last-minute odds 'n ends. Most likely, the store directory at your local **almacén** *(ahl-mah-sen)* did not
department store

look like the one **abajo!** **Usted sabe** that **"niño"** *(neen-yoh)* is Spanish for "<u>child</u>" so if **usted necesita**

something for a child, **usted** would probably look on **piso** *(pee-soh)* **dos, ¿no?**

4. ■ PISO	vajillas efectos eléctricos cristal camas	efectos de domicilio todo para la cocina cerámica lámparas	llavería pasatiempos porcelana pinturas
3. ■ PISO	libros televisores muebles infantiles cochecillos	juguetes instrumentos de música radios	tabaquería café revistas periódicos
2. ■ PISO	especialidades de comida panadería pastelería	ropa de caballero sombreros de dama todo para el niño ropa de dama	servicios al cliente vino alcohol

1. ■ PISO	accesorios para el
	  coche
	ropa interior
	  de dama
		todo para el baño
		zapatos
		oficina de objetos
		  perdidos
			ropa de cama
			todo para deportes
			papelería
			pañuelos

PB	fotografía-óptica sombreros de caballero paraguas	guantes artículos de piel medias relojes	efectos de caballero perfumería confituras joyería

Let's start a checklist **para su** *(soo)* **viaje.** Besides **ropa,** *(roh-pah)* **¿qué necesita usted?** As you learn these
your   clothing

palabras, assemble these items **en un rincón** *(reen-kohn)* of your **casa.** Check **y** make sure that **están**
corner

limpias *(leem-pee-ahs)* **y** ready **para su viaje.** Be sure to do the same **con** *(kohn)* the rest of **las cosas** *(koh-sahs)* that
clean

usted pack. On the next pages, match each item to its picture, draw a line to it and write out

the word many times. As **usted** organize these things, check them off on this list. Do not forget

to take the next group of sticky labels and label these **cosas** *(koh-sahs)* **hoy.** *(oy)*
today

el pasaporte *(pah-sah-por-teh)*
passport

_____ ☐

el billete de avión *(bee-yeh-teh) (ah-vee-ohn)*
ticket

_____ ☐

la maleta *(mah-leh-tah)*
suitcase

_____ ☐

la bolsa *(bohl-sah)*
handbag

la bolsa, la bolsa, la bolsa ✓

la cartera *(kar-teh-rah)*
wallet

_____ ☐

el dinero *(dee-neh-roh)*
money

_____ ☐

las tarjetas de crédito *(tar-heh-tahs) (kreh-dee-toh)*
credit cards

_____ ☐

los cheques de viajero *(cheh-kes) (vee-ah-heh-roh)*
traveler's checks

_____ ☐

la cámara *(kah-mah-rah)*
camera

_____ ☐

el rollo de película *(roh-yoh) (peh-lee-koo-lah)*
film

_____ ☐

el traje de baño *(trah-heh) (bahn-yoh)*
swimsuit

_____ ☐

el traje de baño *(trah-heh) (bahn-yoh)*
swimsuit

_____ ☐

las sandalias *(sahn-dah-lee-ahs)*
sandals

_____ ☐

las gafas de sol *(gah-fahs) (sohl)*
sunglasses

_____ ☐

el cepillo de dientes *(seh-pee-yoh) (dee-en-tes)*
toothbrush

_____ ☐

la pasta de dientes *(pah-stah) (dee-en-tes)*
toothpaste

_____ ☐

el jabón *(hah-bohn)*
soap

_____ ☐

la navaja de afeitar *(nah-vah-hah) (ah-fay-tar)*
razor

_____ ☐

el desodorante *(des-oh-doh-rahn-teh)*
deodorant

_____ ☐

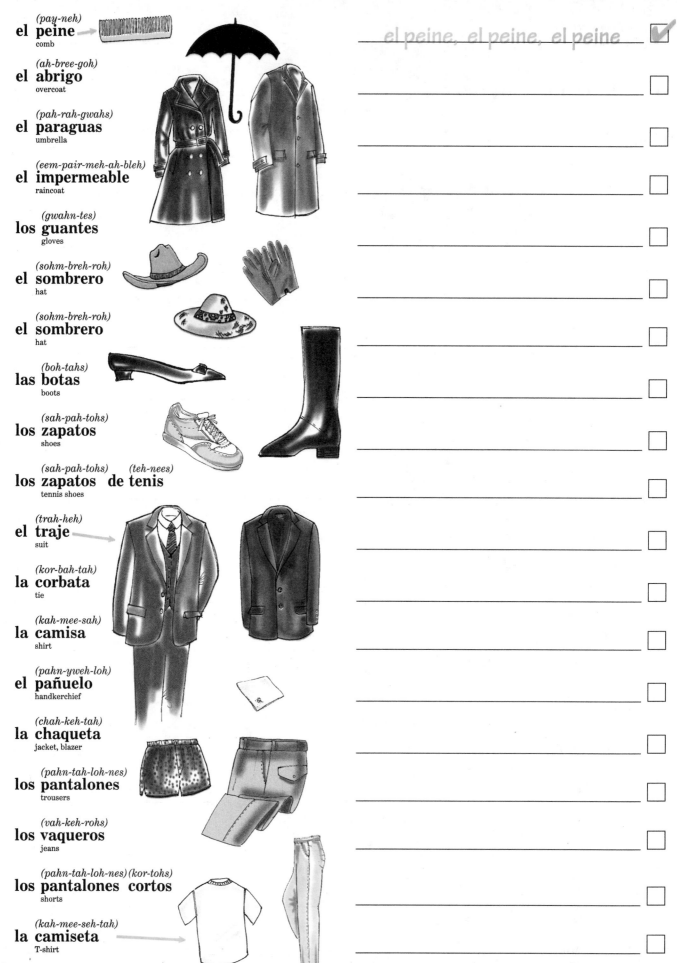

el peine *(pay-neh)*
comb

el peine, el peine, el peine ✓

el abrigo *(ah-bree-goh)*
overcoat

el paraguas *(pah-rah-gwahs)*
umbrella

el impermeable *(eem-pair-meh-ah-bleh)*
raincoat

los guantes *(gwahn-tes)*
gloves

el sombrero *(sohm-breh-roh)*
hat

el sombrero *(sohm-breh-roh)*
hat

las botas *(boh-tahs)*
boots

los zapatos *(sah-pah-tohs)*
shoes

los zapatos de tenis *(sah-pah-tohs) (teh-nees)*
tennis shoes

el traje *(trah-heh)*
suit

la corbata *(kor-bah-tah)*
tie

la camisa *(kah-mee-sah)*
shirt

el pañuelo *(pahn-yweh-loh)*
handkerchief

la chaqueta *(chah-keh-tah)*
jacket, blazer

los pantalones *(pahn-tah-loh-nes)*
trousers

los vaqueros *(vah-keh-rohs)*
jeans

los pantalones cortos *(pahn-tah-loh-nes) (kor-tohs)*
shorts

la camiseta *(kah-mee-seh-tah)*
T-shirt

(kahl-sohn-see-yohs)
los calzoncillos
underpants

☐

(kah-mee-seh-tah)
la camiseta
undershirt

☐

(ves-tee-doh)
el vestido
dress

☐

(bloo-sah)
la blusa
blouse

☐

(fahl-dah)
la falda
skirt

la falda, la falda, la falda ✓

(sweh-tair)
el suéter
sweater

☐

(kohm-bee-nah-see-ohn)
la combinación
slip

☐

(sohs-ten)
el sostén
brassiere

☐

(kahl-sohn-see-yohs)
los calzoncillos
underpants

☐

(kahl-seh-tee-nes)
los calcetines
socks

☐

(meh-dee-ahs)
las medias
pantyhose

☐

(pee-hah-mah)
el pijama
pajamas

☐

(kah-mee-sah) *(dor-meer)*
la camisa de dormir
night   shirt

☐

(bah-tah) *(bahn-yoh)*
la bata de baño
bathrobe

☐

(sah-pah-tee-yahs)
las zapatillas
slippers

☐

From now on, **usted** *(tee-en-eh)* **tiene** *(hah-bohn)* **"jabón" y no** "soap." Having assembled these *(koh-sahs)* **cosas, usted** are
you   have   things

ready **viajar.** Let's add these important shopping phrases to your basic repetoire.
to travel

(keh) *(tah-yah)*
¿Qué talla? _____
what   size

(ah-hoos-teh)
Es un ajuste bueno. _____
it is   good fit

(ah-hoos-teh)
No es un ajuste bueno. _____
it is not   good fit

105

Treat yourself to a final review. **Usted sabe** the names for **tiendas** _(tee-en-dahs)_ **en español,** so let's practice shopping. Just remember your key question **palabras** that you learned in Step 2. Whether **usted** need to buy **sombreros** _(sohm-breh-rohs)_ **o libros** _(lee-brohs)_ the necessary **palabras** are the same.

1. First step — **¿dónde?**

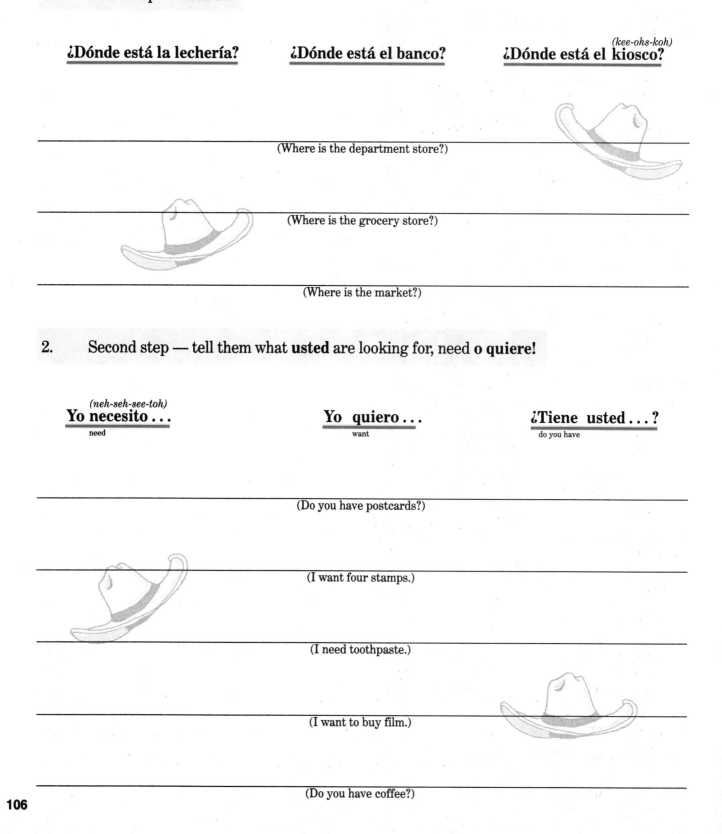

| ¿Dónde está la lechería? | ¿Dónde está el banco? | ¿Dónde está el kiosco? _(kee-ohs-koh)_ |

_____

(Where is the department store?)

_____

(Where is the grocery store?)

_____

(Where is the market?)

2. Second step — tell them what **usted** are looking for, need **o quiere!**

Yo necesito . . . _(neh-seh-see-toh)_ need

Yo quiero . . . want

¿Tiene usted . . . ? do you have

_____

(Do you have postcards?)

_____

(I want four stamps.)

_____

(I need toothpaste.)

_____

(I want to buy film.)

_____

(Do you have coffee?)

Go through the glossary at the end of this **libro y** select **veinte palabras.** *(vain-teh)* Drill the above patterns **con** *(kohn)* these twenty **palabras.** Don't cheat. Drill them **hoy.** *(oy)* **Ahora,** *(ah-oh-rah)* take **veinte** more **palabras de** your glossary **y** do the same.

3. Third step — find out **cuánto cuesta la cosa.** *(kwahn-toh) (kwes-tah) (koh-sah)*

¿Cuánto cuesta esto?	¿Cuánto cuesta un sello? *(say-yoh)*	¿Cuánto cuesta un litro de leche? *(lee-troh) (leh-cheh)*
		liter milk

_____

(How much does the toothpaste cost?)

_____

(How much does the soap cost?)

_____

(How much does a cup of tea cost?)

4.   Fourth step — success! I found it!

Once **usted** find what **usted** would like, **diga,** *(dee-gah)* say

Quiero eso, por favor. *(kee-eh-roh)* _____

or

Dame eso, por favor. *(dah-meh)* _____ Deme usted eso, por favor. _____
give me

O if **usted** would not like it, **diga,**

No quiero eso, gracias. _____

or

No me gusta. *(meh) (goo-stah)* _____
I do not like it

Congratulations! You have finished. By now you should have stuck your labels, flashed your cards, cut out your menu guide and packed your suitcases. You should be very pleased with your accomplishment. You have learned what it sometimes takes others years to achieve and you hopefully had fun doing it. **¡Buen viaje!**

Glossary

This glossary contains words used in this book only. It is not meant to be a dictionary. Consider purchasing a dictionary which best suits your needs - small for traveling, large for reference, or specialized for specific vocabulary needs.

The words here are all presented in alphabetical order followed by the pronunciation guide used in this book.

Remember that Spanish words can change their endings depending upon how they are used. Not all variations are given here, but in many cases you will see "o/a" at the end of a word. This should help you to remember that this word can change its ending. Learn to look for the core of the word.

A

a *(ah)* ....to, at
a la parrilla *(ah)(lah)(pah-rree-yah)* .... grilled
a la Romana *(ah)(lah)(roh-mah-nah)* ....in batter
abajo *(ah-bah-hoh)* .... down, below
abierto/a *(ah-bee-air-toh)* ....open
abra *(ah-brah)* .... open!
abrigo, el *(ah-bree-goh)* ....overcoat
abril *(ah-breel)* ....April
absoluto/a *(ahb-soh-loo-toh)* ....absolute
abuela, la *(ah-bweh-lah)* ....grandmother
abuelo, el *(ah-bweh-loh)* ....grandfather
accidente, el *(ahk-see-den-teh)* ....accident
activo *(ahk-tee-voh)* ....active
acto, el *(ahk-toh)* ....act
acuario, el *(ah-kwar-ee-oh)* ....aquarium
adentro *(ah-den-troh)* ....inside
adiós *(ah-dee-ohs)* ....goodbye
aduana *(ah-doo-ah-nah)* .... customs (at a border)
aeropuerto, el *(ah-eh-roh-pwair-toh)* .... airport
Africa del Sur, la *(ah-free-kah)(del)(soor)* ...... South Africa
agencia de carros de alquiler, la *(ah-hen-see-ah)(deh)(kah-rrohs)* *(deh)(ahl-kee-lair)* ....car-rental agency
agencia de viajes, la *(ah-hen-see-ah)(deh)(vee-ah-hes)* .... travel agency
agosto *(ah-gohs-toh)* ....August
agricultura, la *(ah-gree-kool-too-rah)* .... agriculture
agua, el *(ah-gwah)* .... water
ahora *(ah-or-ah)* ....now
al *(ahl)* .... to the
al centro *(ahl)(sen-troh)* .... to the center
al horno *(ahl)(or-noh)* ....baked
al lado de *(ahl)(lah-doh)(deh)* .... next to
alemán, alemana *(ah-leh-mahn)* .... German
Alemania, la *(ah-leh-mahn-ee-ah)* .... Germany
alfabeto, el *(ahl-fah-beh-toh)* ....alphabet
alfombra, la *(ahl-fohm-brah)* ....carpet
álgebra, el *(ahl-heh-brah)* ....algebra
allí *(ah-yee)* .... there
almacén, el *(ahl-mah-sen)* ....department store
almohada, la *(ah-moh-hah-dah)* ....pillow
almuerzo, el *(ahl-mwair-soh)* .... lunch
alto/a *(ahl-toh)* .... tall, high
amarillo/a *(ah-mah-ree-yoh)* ....yellow
América del Norte *(ah-meh-ree-kah)(del)(nor-teh)* .... North America
América del Sur *(ah-meh-ree-kah)(del)(soor)* ... South America
América Latina *(ah-meh-ree-kah)(lah-tee-nah)* .... Latin America
América *(ah-meh-ree-kah)* ....America
americana, la *(ah-meh-ree-kah-nah)* .... American (female)
americano, el *(ah-meh-ree-kah-noh)* .... American (male)
amigo, el *(ah-mee-goh)* ....friend
anaranjado *('ah-nah-rahn-hah-doh)* ....orange (color)
andar *(ahn-dar)* ....to walk, to go
andén, el *(ahn-den)* ....railway platform
animal, el *(ah-nee-mahl)* .... animal
anual *(ah-noo-ahl)* .... annual

Año Nuevo, el *(ahn-yoh)(nweh-voh)* .... New Year's Day
Año Viejo, el *(ahn-yoh)(vee-eh-hoh)* .... New Year's Eve
año, el *(ahn-yoh)* .... year
aplicación, la *(ah-plee-kah-see-ohn)* ....application
aprender *(ah-pren-dair)* .... to learn
aproximadamente *(ah-prohk-see-mah-dah-men-teh)* ....approximately
aquí *(ah-kee)* .... here
Argentina *(ar-hen-tee-nah)* .... Argentina
armario, el *(ar-mah-ree-oh)* ....cupboard
arriba *(ah-rree-bah)* ....up, above
arte, el *(ar-teh)* ....art
artículos de cuero, los *(ar-tee-koo-lohs)(deh)(kwair-oh)* .... leather goods
artista, el *(ar-tees-tah)* .... artist
asado/a *(ah-sah-doh)* ....roasted
asiento, el *(ah-see-en-toh)* ....seat
aspirina, la *(ah-spee-ree-nah)* .... aspirin
atención, la *(ah-ten-see-ohn)* .... attention
Australia *(ow-strah-lee-ah)* .... Australia
autobús, el *(ow-toh-boos)* .... bus
automóvil, el *(ow-toh-moh-veel)* ....automobile
autopista, la *(ow-toh-pees-tah)* .... freeway
ave, la *(ah-veh)* .... bird, fowl, poultry
avión, el *(ah-vee-ohn)* .... airplane
ayer *(ah-yair)* .... yesterday
azul *(ah-sool)* .... blue
azulejos pintados a mano, los *(ah-soo-leh-hohs)(peen-tah-dos)* *(ah)(mah-noh)* ....hand-painted tiles

B

balcón, el *(bahl-kohn)* .... balcony
banco, el *(bahn-koh)* ....bank
baño, el *(bahn-yoh)* ....bath, bathroom
barato/a *(bah-rah-toh)* ....inexpensive
barco, el *(bar-koh)* .... boat
bata de baño, la *(bah-tah)(deh)(bahn-yoh)* .... bathrobe
batalla, la *(bah-tah-yah)* .... battle
beber *(beh-bair)* .... to drink
bebida, la *(beh-bee-dah)* .... beverage
Bélgica *(bel-hee-kah)* ....Belgium
bicicleta, la *(bee-see-kleh-tah)* .... bicycle
bien *(bee-en)* ....well
biftec, el *(beef-tek)* ....beefsteak
billete, el *(bee-yeh-teh)* .... ticket, banknote, bill
billete de avión, el *(bee-yeh-teh)(deh)(ah-vee-ohn)* ....airplane ticket
billete de teatro, el *(bee-yeh-teh-)(deh)(teh-ah-troh)* .... theater ticket
blanco/a *(blahn-koh)* .... white
blando/a *(blahn-doh)* .... bland
blusa, la *(bloo-sah)* ....blouse
bocadillo, el *(boh-kah-dee-yoh)* .... sandwich, snack
boleto, el *(boh-leh-toh)* ....ticket
boleto sencillo *(boh-leh-toh)(sen-see-yoh)* .... one-way ticket
Bolivia *(boh-lee-vee-ah)* .... Bolivia
bolsa, la *(bohl-sah)* .... purse
botánico *(boh-tah-nee-koh)* .... botanical

botas, las *(boh-tahs)* .... boots
botella, la *(boh-teh-yah)* .... bottle
buen viaje *(bwehn)(vee-ah-heh)* .... have a good trip!
buena suerte *(bweh-nah)(swair-teh)* .... good luck!
buenas noches *(bweh-nahs)(noh-ches)* .... good night
buenas tardes *(bweh-nahs)(tar-des)* .... good afternoon
bueno/a *(bweh-noh)* .... good
buenos días *(bweh-nohs)(dee-ahs)* .. good day, good morning
buzón, el *(boo-sohn)* .... mailbox

C

C = Caballeros *(kah-bah-yair-ohs)* .... gentlemen
caballero, el *(kah-bah-yair-oh)* .... gentleman
cabina de teléfono, la *(kah-bee-nah)(deh)(teh-leh-foh-noh)* ..
.... telephone booth
cabina, la *(kah-bee-nah)* .... booth
cada cuánto *(kah-dah)(kwahn-toh)* .... how often
café con leche *(kah-feh)(kohn)(leh-cheh)* ... coffee with milk
café, el *(kah-feh)* .... coffee, coffeehouse
cajero, el *(kah-heh-roh)* .... cashier
calcetines, los *(kahl-seh-tee-nes)* .... socks
cálculo, el *(kahl-koo-loh)* .... calculation
calendario, el *(kah-len-dah-ree-oh)* .... calendar
caliente *(kah-lee-en-teh)* .... hot
calle, la *(kah-yeh)* .... street
calma, la *(kahl-mah)* .... calm
calor, el *(kah-lor)* .... heat
calzoncillos, los *(kahl-sohn-see-yohs)* .... underpants
cama, la *(kah-mah)* .... bed
cámara, la *(kah-mah-rah)* .... camera
camarera, la *(kah-mah-reh-rah)* .... waitress
camarero, el *(kah-mah-reh-roh)* .... waiter
cambiar *(kahm-bee-ar)* ..... to transfer, to exchange money
cambio, el *(kahm-bee-oh)* .... change
camino, el *(kah-mee-noh)* .... road
camisa, la *(kah-mee-sah)* .... shirt
camisa de dormir, la *(kah-mee-sah)(deh)(dor-meer)* .. nightshirt
camiseta, la *(kah-mee-seh-tah)* .... undershirt, T-shirt
Canadá *(kah-nah-dah)* .... Canada
canadiense *(kah-nah-dee-en-seh)* .... Canadian
cantina, la *(kahn-tee-nah)* .... bar
capital, la *(kah-pee-tahl)* .... capital
carácter, el *(kah-rahk-tair)* .... character
carne, la *(kar-neh)* .... meat
carnero *(kar-neh-roh)* .... mutton
carnicería, la *(kar-nee-seh-ree-ah)* .... butcher shop
caro/a *(kah-roh)* .... expensive
carretera, la *(kar-rreh-tair-ah)* .... freeway
carro, el *(kah-rroh)* .... car
carro de alquiler, el *(kar-rroh)(deh)(ahl-kee-lair)* .. rental car
carta, la *(kar-tah)* .... menu, letter
cartera, la *(kar-teh-rah)* .... wallet
casa, la *(kah-sah)* .... house
castillo, el *(kahs-tee-yoh)* .... castle
catedral, la *(kah-teh-drahl)* .... cathedral
católico/a *(kah-toh-lee-koh)* .... Catholic
catorce *(kah-tor-seh)* .... fourteen
causa, la *(kow-sah)* .... cause
caza, la *(kah-sah)* .... game (food)
ceder el paso *(seh-dair)(el)(pah-soh)* .... yield (traffic)
cena, la *(sehn-ah)* .... supper, evening meal
centígrado *(sen-tee-grah-doh)* .... Centigrade
centro, el *(sen-troh)* .... center, middle
cepillo de dientes, el *(seh-pee-yoh)(deh)(dee-en-tes)* .. toothbrush
cerámica, la *(seh-rah-mee-kah)* .... ceramics
cerdo, el *(sair-doh)* .... pork
cero *(seh-roh)* .... zero
cerrado/a *(seh-rrah-doh)* .... closed
cerveza, la *(sair-veh-sah)* .... beer
cesto para papeles, el *(ses-toh)(pah-rah)(pah-peh-les)* .....
.... wastebasket
chaqueta, la *(chah-keh-tah)* .... jacket
cheque, el *(cheh-keh)* .... check

cheques de viajero, las *(cheh-kes)(deh)(vee-ah-heh-roh)* ...
.... traveler's checks
Chile *(chee-leh)* .... Chile
chino, el *(chee-noh)* .... Chinese
chocolate, el *(choh-koh-lah-teh)* .... chocolate, cocoa
cien *(see-en)* .... hundred
ciento *(see-en-toh)* .... hundred
cinco *(see-koh)* .... five
cinco mil *(seen-koh)(meel)* .... five thousand
cincuenta *(seen-kwen-tah)* .... fifty
cine, el *(see-neh)* .... cinema
círculo, el *(seer-koo-loh)* .... circle
civilización, la *(see-vee-lee-sah-see-ohn)* .... civilization
clase, la *(klah-seh)* .... class
coche, el *(koh-cheh)* .... car
coche-cama, el *(koh-cheh-kah-mah)* .... sleeping car
coche-comedor, el *(koh-cheh-koh-meh-dor)* ..... dining car
cocido/a *(koh-see-doh)* .... cooked
cocido/a al vapor *(koh-see-doh)(ahl)(vah-por)* ..... steamed
cocina, la *(koh-see-nah)* .... kitchen/stove
colección, la *(koh-lek-see-ohn)* .... collection
Colombia *(koh-lohm-bee-ah)* .... Colombia
color, el *(koh-lor)* .... color
combinación, la *(kohm-bee-nah-see-ohn)* .. combination, slip
comedor, el *(koh-meh-dor)* .... dining room
comenzar *(koh-men-sar)* .... to begin, to commence
comer *(koh-mair)* .... to eat
cómico/a *(koh-mee-koh)* .... comical
comida, la *(koh-mee-dah)* .... meal, dinner
¿cómo? *(koh-moh)* .... how?
¿Cómo está? *(koh-moh)(es-tah)* .... How are you?
¿Cómo está usted? *(koh-moh)(es-tah)(oos-ted)* .. How are you?
¿Cómo se llama? *(koh-moh)(seh)(yah-mah)* ....
.... What is your name? How are you called?
compañía, la *(kohm-pahn-yee-ah)* .... company
compartimiento, el *(kohm-par-tee-mee-en-toh)* .. compartment
complicado/a *(kohm-plee-kah-doh)* .... complicated
comprar *(kohm-prar)* .... to buy
comprender *(kohm-pren-dair)* .... to understand
computadora, la *(kohm-poo-tah-dor-ah)* .... computer
comunicación, la *(koh-moo-nee-kah-see-ohn)* .. communication
con *(kohn)* .... with
¿Con quién? *(kohn)(kee-en)* .... With whom?
¿Con quién hablo yo? *(kohn)(kee-en)(ah-bloh)(yoh)* ....
.... With whom am I speaking?
concierto, el *(kohn-see-air-toh)* .... concert
condición, la *(kohn-dee-see-ohn)* .... condition
conversación, la *(kohn-vair-sah-see-ohn)* ..... conversation
conversación telefónica, la *(kohn-vair-sah-see-oh)(teh-leh-foh-nee-kah)* .... telephone conversation
corbata, la *(kor-bah-tah)* .... necktie
cordero, el *(kor-deh-roh)* .... lamb
correcto/a *(koh-rrek-toh)* .... correct
correo aéreo, el *(koh-rreh-oh)(ah-eh-reh-oh)* ... airmail
correo, el *(koh-rreh-oh)* .... mail
corrida de toros, la *(koh-rree-dah)(deh)(toh-rohs)* .. bullfight
cortina, la *(kor-tee-nah)* .... curtain
corto/a *(kor-toh)* .... short
cosa, la *(koh-sah)* .... thing
costa del este, la *(koh-stah)(del)(es-teh)* .... east coast
costa del oeste, la *(koh-stah)(del)(oh-es-teh)* ..... west coast
Costa Rica *(koh-stah)(ree-kah)* .... Costa Rica
costar *(koh-star)* .... to cost
costumbre hispana, la *(kohs-toom-breh)(ees-pah-nah)* .....
.... Hispanic custom
crema, la *(kreh-mah)* .... cream
croissant, el *(kwah-sahnt)* .... croissant
¿cuál? *(kwahl)* .... which?
¿cuándo? *(kwahn-doh)* .... when?
¿cuántos/as? *(kwahn-tohs)* .... how many?
¿cuánto/a? *(kwahn-toh)* .... how much?
¿Cuánto cuesta? *(kwahn-toh)(kwes-tah)* ....
.... How much does it cost?
cuarenta *(kwah-ren-tah)* .... forty **109**

cuarto *(kwar-toh)* .... quarter (time)
cuarto, el *(kwar-toh)* .... room
cuatro *(kwah-troh)* .... four
cuatro mil *(kwah-troh)(meel)* .... four thousand
Cuba, la *(koo-bah)* .... Cuba
cubierto, el *(koo-bee-air-toh)* .... special meal of the day
cuchara, la *(koo-chah-rah)* .... spoon
cuchillo, el *(koo-chee-yoh)* .... knife
cuenta, la *(kwehn-tah)* .... bill
cultura, la *(kool-too-rah)* .... culture

D

D = Damas *(dah-mahs)* .... ladies
dama, la *(dah-mah)* .... lady
¡dame! *(dah-meh)* .... give me!
¡Dame eso, por favor! *(dah-meh)(eh-soh)(por)(fah-vor)* ....
give me that please!
de *(deh)* .... of, from
de barril *(deh)(bah-rreel)* .... draught
de nada *(deh)(nah-dah)* .... it's nothing, don't mention it
debajo *(deh-bah-hoh)* .... under, below
decente *(deh-sen-teh)* .... decent
decir *(deh-seer)* .... to say
decisión, la *(deh-see-see-ohn)* .... decision
declaración, la *(deh-klah-rah-see-ohn)* .... declaration
del *(del)* .... of the, from the
delante de *(deh-lahn-teh)(deh)* .... in front of
depender *(deh-pen-dair)* .... to depend
derecha *(deh-reh-chah)* .... right
derecho *(deh-reh-choh)* .... straight ahead
desayuno, el *(deh-sah-yoo-noh)* .... breakfast
desgracia, la *(des-grah-see-ah)* .... disgrace
desodorante, el *(des-oh-doh-rahn-teh)* ..... deodorant
despacio *(des-pah-see-oh)* .... slowly
despertador, el *(des-pair-tah-dor)* .... alarm clock
desvío, el *(des-vee-oh)* .... detour
detrás de *(deh-trahs)(deh)* .... behind
día, el *(dee-ah)* .... day
Día del Trabajo, el *(dee-ah)(del)(trah-bah-hoh)* . Labor Day
diccionario, el *(deek-see-oh-nar-ee-oh)* .... dictionary
dice *(dee-seh)* .... (he, she) says
diciembre *(dee-see-em-breh)* .... December
diecinueve *(dee-eh-see-nweh-veh)* .... nineteen
dieciocho *(dee-eh-see-oh-choh)* .... eighteen
dieciséis *(dee-eh-see-sehs)* .... sixteen
diecisiete, *(dee-eh-see-see-eh-teh)* .... seventeen
diez *(dee-es)* .... ten
diez mil *(dee-es)(meel)* .... ten thousand
diez mil quinientos *(dee-es)(meel)(kee-nee-en-tohs)* ....
.... ten thousand five hundred
diferencia, la *(dee-feh-ren-see-ah)* .... difference
difícil *(dee-fee-seel)* .... difficult
¡diga! *(dee-gah)* .... say!
dinero, el *(dee-nah-roh)* .... money
dirección, la *(dee-rek-see-ohn)* .... direction, address
distancia, la *(dees-tahn-see-ah)* .... distance
división, la *(dee-vee-see-ohn)* .... division
¡doble usted! *(doh-bleh)(oos-ted)* .... turn!
doce *(doh-seh)* .... twelve
doctor, el *(dohk-tor)* .... doctor
documento, el *(doh-koo-men-toh)* .... document
dólar, el *(doh-lar)* .... dollar
domingo, el *(doh-meen-goh)* .... Sunday
¿dónde? *(dohn-deh)* .... where?
dormir *(dor-meer)* .... to sleep
dormitorio, el *(dor-mee-tor-ee-oh)* .... bedroom
dos *(dohs)* .... two
dos mil *(dohs)(meel)* .... two thousand
doscientos *(dohs-see-en-tohs)* .... two hundred
ducha, la *(doo-chah)* .... shower
durar *(doo-rar)* .... to last

E

economía, la *(eh-koh-noh-mee-ah)* .... economy
Ecuador *(eh-kwah-dor)* .... Ecuador
ejemplo, el *(eh-hem-ploh)* .... example
el *(el)* .... the (masculine singular)
él *(el)* .... he
eléctrico/a *(eh-lek-tree-koh)* .... electric
ella *(eh-yah)* .... she
ellas *(eh-yahs)* .... they (feminine)
ellos *(eh-yohs)* .... they (masculine or mixed)
empujar *(em-poo-har)* .... push (doors)
en *(en)* .... into, in, on, at
en español *(en)(es-pahn-yohl)* .... in Spanish
encontrar *(en-kohn-trar)* .... to find
eneldo *(eh-nel-doh)* .... dill
enero *(eh-neh-roh)* .... January
enfermo/a *(en-fair-moh)* .... sick
enorme *(eh-nor-meh)* .... enormous
ensalada, la *(en-sah-lah-dah)* .... salad
entrada, la *(en-trah-dah)* .... entrance
entrada principal, la *(en-trah-dah)(preen-see-pahl)* ......
.... main entrance
entrar *(en-trar)* .... to enter
entre *(en-treh)* .... between
entremeses, los *(en-treh-meh-ses)* .... appetizers
error, el *(eh-rror)* .... error
es *(es)* .... is, it is
es muy importante *(es)(mwee)(eem-por-tahn-teh)* ....
.... it is very important
es un ajuste bueno *(es)(oon)(ah-hoos-teh)(bweh-noh)* ......
.... it is a good fit
escribir *(es-kree-beer)* .... to write
escritorio, el *(es-kree-tor-ee-oh)* .... desk
escuela, la *(es-kweh-lah)* .... school
eso/a *(eh-soh)* .... that
España *(es-pahn-yah)* .... Spain
español, el *(es-pahn-yohl)* .... Spanish
espejo, el *(es-peh-hoh)* .... mirror
espléndido/a *(es-plen-dee-doh)* .... splendid
está *(es-tah)* .... (you, he, she) is/are
estación, la *(es-tah-see-ohn)* .... station
estación de servicio, la *(es-tah-see-ohn)(deh)(sair-vee-see-oh)*
.... service station
estación de tren, la *(es-tah-see-ohn)(deh)(tren)* .. train station
estacionamiento, el *(es-tah-see-oh-nah-mee-en-toh)* .. parking lot
estadio, el *(es-tah-dee-oh)* .... stadium
estado, el *(es-tah-doh)* .... state
Estados Unidos, los *(es-tah-dohs)(oo-nee-dohs)* ....
.... the United States
están *(es-tahn)* .... (they) are
este, el *(es-teh)* .... east
esto/a *(es-toh)* .... this, this one
estoy *(es-toy)* .... (I) am
estudiante, el *(es-too-dee-ahn-teh)* .... student
Europa *(eh-oo-roh-pah)* .... Europe
exacto *(ek-sahk-toh)* .... exact
excelente *(ek-seh-len-teh)* .... excellent
excusado, el *(es-koo-sah-doh)* .... toilet
existir *(ek-sees-teer)* .... to exist
expresión, la *(es-preh-see-ohn)* .... expression
extranjero *(es-trahn-heh-roh)* .... foreign, international
extremo/aa *(es-treh-moh)* .... extreme

F

Fahrenheit *(fah-ren-hite)* .... Fahrenheit
falda, la *(fahl-dah)* .... skirt
fama, la *(fah-mah)* .... fame
familia, la *(fah-mee-lee-ah)* .... family
famoso/a *(fah-moh-soh)* .... famous
farmacia, la *(far-mah-see-ah)* .... pharmacy, drugstore
favor, el *(fah-vor)* .... favor
fax, el *(fahks)* .... fax, facsimile
febrero, el *(feh-breh-roh)* .... February

ficción, la *(feek-see-ohn)*	fiction
figura, la *(fee-goo-rah)*	figure
final *(fee-nahl)*	final
firma, la *(feer-mah)*	signature
flor, la *(flor)*	flower
florería, la *(floh-reh-ree-ah)*	flower shop
floresta, la *(floh-res-tah)*	woods
fonda, la *(fohn-dah)*	inn
forma, la *(for-mah)*	form
fortuna, la *(for-too-nah)*	fortune
foto, la *(foh-toh)*	photo
francés, el *(frahn-ses)*	French
Francia *(frahn-see-ah)*	France
frase siguiente, la *(frah-seh)(see-gee-en-teh)*	following phrase
frecuente *(freh-kwen-teh)*	frequent
frío/a *(free-oh)*	cold
frito/a *(free-toh)*	fried
fruta, la *(froo-tah)*	fruit
fue *(fweh)*	was
fugitivo, el *(foo-hee-tee-voh)*	fugitive
futuro, el *(foo-too-roh)*	future

G

gafas de sol, las *(gah-fahs)(deh)(sohl)*	sunglasses
gafas, las *(gah-fahs)*	eyeglasses
garaje, el *(gah-rah-heh)*	garage
gasolina, la *(gah-soh-lee-nah)*	gasoline
gato, el *(gah-toh)*	cat
gloria, la *(glor-ee-ah)*	glory
gracias *(grah-see-ahs)*	thanks
grado, el *(grah-doh)*	degree
grande *(grahn-deh)*	large
gratis *(grah-tees)*	free, no charge
grave *(grah-veh)*	grave, serious
gris *(grees)*	gray
grupo, el *(groo-poh)*	group
guantes, los *(gwahn-tes)*	gloves
guardar *(gwar-dar)*	to guard, to keep
Guatemala *(gwah-teh-mah-lah)*	Guatemala
guía telefónica, la *(gee-ah)(teh-leh-foh-nee-kah)*	telephone book

H

habitual *(ah-bee-too-ahl)*	habitual
hablar *(ah-blar)*	to speak
hace buen tiempo *(ah-seh)(bwehn)(tee-em-poh)*	it's good weather
hace mal tiempo *(ah-seh)(mahl)(tee-em-poh)*	it's bad weather
hacer *(ah-sair)*	to make, to do
hacer la maleta *(ah-sair)(lah)(mah-leh-tah)*	to pack
hasta luego *(ah-stah)(lweh-goh)*	until then
hasta mañana *(ah-stah)(mahn-yah-nah)*	until tomorrow
hay *(ah-ee)*	there is, there are
hermana, la *(air-mah-nah)*	sister
hermano, el *(air-mah-noh)*	brother
hielo, el *(ee-eh-loh)*	ice
hija, la *(ee-hah)*	daughter
hijo, el *(ee-hoh)*	son
historia, la *(ees-toh-ree-ah)*	history
¡hola! *(oh-lah)*	hi!
hombre, el *(ohm-breh)*	man
Honduras *(ohn-doo-rahs)*	Honduras
honesto/a *(oh-nes-toh)*	honest
honor, el *(oh-nor)*	honor
horario, el *(oh-rah-ree-oh)*	schedule, timetable
horno, el *(or-noh)*	oven
hotel, el *(oh-tel)*	hotel
hoy *(oy)*	today
huevo pasado por aqua, el *(oo-eh-voh)(pah-sah-oh)(por)(ah-gwah)*	soft-boiled egg
huevo, el *(oo-eh-voh)*	egg
humor, el *(oo-mor)*	humor

I

ida y vuelta, la *(ee-dah)(ee)(vwel-tah)*	round trip
idea, la *(ee-deh-ah)*	idea
iglesia, la *(ee-gleh-see-ah)*	church
imaginación, la *(ee-mah-hee-nah-see-ohn)*	imagination
impermeable, el *(eem-pair-meh-ah-bleh)*	raincoat
importancia, la *(eem-por-tahn-see-ah)*	importance
importante *(eem-por-tahn-teh)*	important
imposible *(eem-poh-see-bleh)*	impossible
incendio, el *(een-sen-dee-oh)*	fire
incluido/a *(een-kloo-ee-doh)*	included
incorrecto/a *(een-koh-rrek-toh)*	incorrect
influencia, la *(een-floo-en-see-ah)*	influence
información, la *(een-for-mah-see-ohn)*	information
Inglaterra *(een-glah-teh-rrah)*	England
inglés *(een-gles)*	English
instrucción, la *(een-strook-see-ohn)*	instruction
instrumento, el *(een-stroo-men-toh)*	instrument
inteligencia, la *(een-teh-lee-hen-see-ah)*	intelligence
intención, la *(een-ten-see-ohn)*	intention
interesante *(een-teh-reh-sahn-teh)*	interesting
interior, el *(een-teh-ree-or)*	interior
invierno, el *(een-vee-air-noh)*	winter
invitar *(een-vee-tar)*	to invite
ir *(eer)*	to go
ir en coche *(eer)(en)(koh-cheh)*	to drive, to go by car
Irlanda del Norte *(eer-lahn-dah)(del)(nor-teh)*	Northern Ireland
Italia *(ee-tah-lee-ah)*	Italy
italiano/a *(ee-tah-lee-ah-noh)*	Italian
izquierda *(ees-kee-air-day)*	left

J

jabón, el *(hah-bohn)*	soap
japonés, el *(hah-poh-nes)*	Japanese
jardín, el *(har-deen)*	garden
joven *(hoh-ven)*	young
joyas, las *(hoh-yahs)*	jewelry
judío/a *(hoo-dee-oh)*	Jewish
jueves, el *(hoo-eh-ves)*	Thursday
jugo, el *(hoo-goh)*	juice
jugo de manzana, el *(hoo-goh)(deh)(mahn-zah-nah)*	apple juice
jugo de naranja, el *(hoo-goh)(deh)(nah-rahn-hah)*	orange juice
jugo de tomate, el *(hoo-goh)(deh)(toh-mah-teh)*	tomato juice
jugo de toronja, el *(hoo-goh)(deh)(toh-rohn-hah)*	grapefruit juice
julio *(hoo-lee-oh)*	July
junio *(hoo-nee-oh)*	June
justicia, la *(hoos-tee-see-ah)*	justice
juvenil *(hoo-veh-neel)*	juvenile

K

kilómetro, el *(kee-loh-meh-troh)*	kilometer
kiosco, el *(kee-ohs-koh)*	newsstand

L

la *(lah)*	the (feminine singular)
lámpara, la *(lahm-pah-rah)*	lamp
lápiz, el *(lah-pees)*	pencil
largo/a *(lar-goh)*	long
las *(lahs)*	the (feminine plural)
latín, el *(lah-teen)*	Latin
lavabo, el *(lah-vah-boh)*	washstand
lavandería, la *(lah-vahn-deh-ree-ah)*	laundry
lavar *(lah-var)*	to wash
lección, la *(lek-see-ohn)*	lesson
leche, la *(leh-cheh)*	milk
lechería, la *(leh-cheh-ree-ah)*	dairy
leer *(leh-air)*	to read
legal *(leh-gahl)*	legal

legumbre, la *(leh-goom-breh)* . . . . vegetable
libre *(lee-breh)* . . . . free
librería, la *(lee-breh-ree-ah)* . . . . bookstore
libro, el *(lee-broh)* . . . . book
licor, el *(lee-kor)* . . . . liquor
límite de velocidad, el *(lee-mee-teh)(deh)(veh-loh-see-dahd)*
. . . . speed limit
limón, el *(lee-mohn)* . . . . lemon
limonada, la *(lee-moh-nah-dah)* . . . . lemonade
limpio/a *(leem-pee-oh)* . . . . clean
línea, la *(lee-neh-ah)* . . . . line
lista, la *(lees-tah)* . . . . list
litro, el *(lee-troh)* . . . . liter
llamada de larga distancia, la *(yah-mah-dah)(deh)(lar-gah)*
(dees-tahn-see-ah) . . . . long-distance telephone call
llamada internaciónale, la *(yah-mah-dah)(een-tair-nah-see-*
oh-nah-leh) . . . . international telephone call
llamada local, la *(yah-mah-dah)(loh-kahl)* . . local telephone call
llamar *(yah-mar)* . . . . to call
llegada, la *(yeh-gah-dah)* . . . . arrival
llegar *(yeh-gar)* . . . . to arrive
llueve *(yweh-veh)* . . . . it rains
lo siento *(loh)(see-en-toh)* . . . . I'm sorry
local *(loh-kahl)* . . . . local
los *(lohs)* . . . . the (masculine plural and mixed plural)
luego *(lweh-goh)* . . . . then
lunes, el *(loo-nes)* . . . . Monday

M

madre, la *(mah-dreh)* . . . . mother
mágico/a *(mah-hee-koh)* . . . . magic
magnífico/a *(mahg-nee-fee-koh)* . . . . magnificent
maleta, la *(mah-leh-tah)* . . . . suitcase
malo/a *(mah-loh)* . . . . bad
mandar *(mahn-dar)* . . . . to send
manta, la *(mahn-tah)* . . . . blanket
mantequilla, la *(mahn-teh-kee-yah)* . . . . butter
manzana, la *(mahn-zah-nah)* . . . . apple
mañana *(mahn-yah-nah)* . . . . tomorrow
mañana, la *(mahn-yah-nah)* . . . . morning
mapa, el *(mah-pah)* . . . . map
mar, el *(mar)* . . . . sea
Mar Mediterráneo, el *(mar)(meh-dee-tair-rah-neh-oh)* . . . .
. . . . Mediterranean Sea
marca, la *(mar-kah)* . . . . mark
mariachis, los *(mah-ree-ah-chees)* . . . . . Mexican street band
marrón *(mah-rrohn)* . . . . brown
martes, el *(mar-tes)* . . . . Tuesday
marzo *(mar-soh)* . . . . March
más *(mahs)* . . . . more
masculino/a *(mahs-koo-lee-noh)* . . . . masculine
matemáticas, las *(mah-teh-mah-tee-kahs)* . . . . mathematics
matrimonio, el *(mah-tree-moh-nee-oh)* . . . . matrimony
mayo *(mah-yoh)* . . . . May
me llamo *(meh)(yah-moh)* . . . . . my name is, I am called
mecánico/a *(meh-kah-nee-koh)* . . . . mechanical
medias, las *(meh-dee-ahs)* . . . . stockings
medicina, la *(meh-dee-see-nah)* . . . . medicine
médico, el *(meh-dee-koh)* . . . . doctor
medio, el *(meh-dee-oh)* . . . . half
melodía, la *(meh-loh-dee-ah)* . . . . melody
menos *(meh-nohs)* . . . . minus
menos cuarto *(meh-nohs)(kwar-toh)* . . . . . quarter to (time)
menú, el *(meh-noo)* . . . . menu
mercado, el *(mair-kah-doh)* . . . . market
mermelada, la *(mair-meh-lah-dah)* . . . . . jam, marmalade
mes, el *(mehs)* . . . . month
mesa, la *(meh-sah)* . . . . table
mesera, la *(meh-sair-ah)* . . . . waitress
mesero, el *(meh-sair-oh)* . . . . waiter
metro, el *(meh-troh)* . . . . subway, meter
metropolitano/a *(meh-troh-poh-lee-tah-noh)* . . metropolitan
México, el *(meh-hee-koh)* . . . . Mexico
mi *(mee)* . . . . my

¡Mi casa es su casa! *(mee)(kah-sah)(es)(soo)(kah-sah)* . . . .
. . . . my home is your home
miércoles, el *(mee-air-koh-les)* . . . . Wednesday
mil *(meel)* . . . . thousand
mínimo, el *(mee-nee-moh)* . . . . minimum
ministro, el *(mee-nees-troh)* . . . . minister
minuto, el *(mee-noo-toh)* . . . . minute
moderno/a *(moh-dair-noh)* . . . . modern
momento, el *(moh-men-toh)* . . . . moment
monarquía, la *(moh-nar-kee-ah)* . . . . monarchy
monasterio, el *(moh-nahs-teh-ree-oh)* . . . . monastery
moneda, la *(moh-neh-dah)* . . . . coin (money)
montaña, la *(mohn-tahn-yah)* . . . . mountain
motocicleta, la *(moh-toh-see-kleh-tah)* . . . . . . motorcycle
muchas gracias *(moo-chahs)(grah-see-ahs))* . . many thanks
mucho/a *(moo-choh)* . . . . much, a lot
multicolor *(mool-tee-koh-lor)* . . . . multi-colored
museo, el *(moo-seh-oh)* . . . . museum
música, la *(moo-see-kah)* . . . . music
muy *(mwee)* . . . . very
muy importante *(mwee)(eem-por-tahn-teh)* . . very important

N

nación, la *(nah-see-ohn)* . . . . nation
nada *(nah-dah)* . . . . nothing
naranja *(nah-rahn-hah)* . . . . orange (fruit)
natural *(nah-too-rahl)* . . . . natural
navaja de afeitar, la *(nah-vah-hah)(deh)(ah-fay-tar)* . . .razor
Navidad, la *(nah-vee-dahd)* . . . . Christmas
necesario/a *(neh-seh-sah-ree-oh)* . . . . necessary
necesitar *(neh-seh-see-tar)* . . . . to need
negro/a *(neh-groh)* . . . . black
niebla, la *(nee-eh-blah)* . . . . fog
nieva *(nee-eh-vah)* . . . . it snows
niña, la *(neen-yah)* . . . . girl
niño, el *(neen-yoh)* . . . . boy
no *(noh)* . . . . no, not
no entrar *(noh)(en-trar)* . . . . no entrance
no es un ajuste bueno *(noh)(es)(oon)(ah-hoos-teh)(bweh-noh)*
. . . . it is not a good fit
no me gusta *(noh)(meh)(goos-tah)* . . . .
. . . . I don't like it, it doesn't please me
noche, la *(noh-cheh)* . . . . night
Nochebuena, la *(noh-cheh-bweh-nah)* . . . . . . Christmas Eve
nombre, el *(nohm-breh)* . . . . name
normal *(nor-mahl)* . . . . normal
norte, el *(nor-teh)* . . . . north
nosotros *(noh-soh-trohs)* . . . . we
noticia, la *(noh-tee-see-ah)* . . . . notice
noventa *(noh-ven-tah)* . . . . ninety
noviembre *(noh-vee-em-breh)* . . . . November
nueve *(nweh-veh)* . . . . nine
nueve mil *(nweh-veh)(meel)* . . . . nine thousand
nuevo/a *(nweh-voh)* . . . . new
número, el *(noo-meh-roh)* . . . . number

O

o *(oh)* . . . . or
objeto, el *(ohb-heh-toh)* . . . . object
ocasión, la *(oh-kah-see-ohn)* . . . . occasion
occidente, el *(ohk-see-den-teh)* . . . . accident, west
océano, el *(oh-seh-ah-noh)* . . . . ocean
ochenta *(oh-chen-tah)* . . . . eighty
ocho *(oh-choh)* . . . . eight
ocho mil *(oh-choh)(meel)* . . . . eight thousand
octubre *(ohk-too-breh)* . . . . October
ocupado/a *(oh-koo-pah-doh)* . . . . occupied, busy
oeste, el *(oh-es-teh)* . . . . west
oficina, la *(oh-fee-see-nah)* . . . . office, study
oficina de cambio, la *(oh-fee-see-nah)(deh)(kahm-bee-oh)* . .
. . . . money-exchange office
oficina de correos, la *(oh-fee-see-nah)(deh)(koh-rreh-ohs)* . .
. . . . post office

oficina de objetos perdidos, la *(oh-fee-see-nah)(deh)(ohb-heh-tohs) (pair-dee-dohs)* .... lost-and-found office
oliva, la *(oh-lee-vah)* .... olive
once *(ohn-seh)* .... eleven
once mil *(ohn-seh)(meel)* .... eleven thousand
ópera, la *(oh-peh-rah)* .... opera
operación, la *(oh-peh-rah-see-ohn)* .... operation
operadora, la *(oh-pair-ah-dor-ah)* .... operator
oportunidad, la *(oh-por-too-nee-dahd)* .... opportunity
oposición, la *(oh-poh-see-see-ohn)* ...... opposition
ordinario/a *(or-dee-nah-ree-oh)* .... ordinary
oriental *(oh-ree-en-tahl)* .... oriental
original *(oh-ree-hee-nahl)* .... original
otoño, el *(oh-tohn-yoh)* .... autumn
oxígeno, el *(ohk-see-heh-noh)* .... oxygen

P

padre, el *(pah-dreh)* .... father
pagar *(pah-gar)* .... to pay
página, la *(pah-hee-nah)* .... page
país, el *(pah-ees)* .... country
palabra, la *(pah-lah-brah)* .... word
palacio, el *(pah-lah-see-oh)* .... palace
palma, la *(pahl-mah)* .... palm
pan, el *(pahn)* .... bread
panadería, la *(pah-nah-deh-ree-ah)* ..... bakery
Panamá, la *(pah-nah-mah)* .... Panama
panecillo, el *(pah-neh-see-yoh)* .... roll (bread)
pánico, el *(pah-nee-koh)* .... panic
pantalones, los *(pahn-tah-loh-nes)* ...... trousers
pantalones cortos, los *(pahn-tah-loh-nes)(kor-tohs)* .. shorts
pañuelo, el *(pahn-yweh-loh)* .... handkerchief
papel, el *(pah-pel)* .... paper
papelería, la *(pah-peh-leh-ree-ah)* ... stationery store
paquete, el *(pah-keh-teh)* .... package
para *(pah-rah)* .... for
parada, la *(pah-rah-dah)* .... stop
parada de autobús, la *(pah-rah-dah)(deh)(ow-toh-boos)* ....
.... bus stop
parada del metro, la *(pah-rah-dah)(del)(meh-troh)* ....
.... subway stop
parada del tranvía, la *(pah-rah-dah)(del)(trahn-vee-ah)* ...
.... streetcar stop
parador, el *(pah-rah-dor)* .... inn
paraguas, el *(pah-rah-gwahs)* .... umbrella
Paraguay *(pah-rah-gwhy)* .... Paraguay
¡pare! *(pah-reh)* .... stop!
parientes, los *(pah-ree-en-tes)* .... relatives
parque, el *(par-keh)* .... park
partida, la *(par-tee-dah)* .... departure
partir *(par-teer)* .... to depart
pasa *(pah-sah)* .... happens (as in ¿Qué pasa?)
pasaporte, el *(pah-sah-por-teh)* .... passport
Pascua, la *(pahs-kwah)* .... Easter
pasta, la *(pah-stah)* .... pasta, paste
pasta de dientes, la *(pah-stah)(deh)(dee-en-tes)* .. toothpaste
pastel, el *(pahs-tel)* .... pastry
pastelería, la *(pahs-teh-leh-ree-ah)* ... pastry shop
pausa, la *(pow-sah)* .... pause
pedir *(peh-deer)* .... to order, to request
peine, el *(pay-neh)* .... comb
película, la *(peh-lee-koo-lah)* .... film
peluquería, la *(peh-loo-keh-ree-ah)* ... hairdresser's
pensión, la *(pehn-see-ohn)* ..... boarding house, small hotel
pequeño/a *(peh-kehn-yoh)* .... small
pera, la *(peh-rah)* .... pear
perder *(peh-deer)* .... to lose
perdón, el *(pair-dohn)* .... pardon me, excuse me
perdóneme *(pair-doh-neh-meh)* .... pardon, excuse me
perfecto/a *(pair-fek-toh)* .... perfect
perfume, el *(pair-foo-meh)* .... perfume
periódico, el *(peh-ree-oh-dee-koh)* ... newspaper
perro, el *(peh-rroh)* .... dog
persona, la *(pair-soh-nah)* .... person

Perú *(peh-roo)* .... Peru
pescadería, la *(pes-kah-deh-ree-ah)* .... fish store
pescado, el *(pes-kah-doh)* .... fish
peso, el *(peh-soh)* .... unit of Mexican currency
piano, el *(pee-ah-noh)* .... piano
pijama, el *(pee-hah-mah)* .... pajamas
pimienta, la *(pee-mee-en-tah)* .... pepper
pintura, la *(peen-toor-ah)* .... picture, painting
planta baja (PB), la *(plahn-tah)(bah-hah)* .... ground floor
plato, el *(plah-toh)* .... plate
playa, la *(plah-yah)* .... beach
plaza, la *(plah-sah)* .... plaza
Plaza de Toros, la *(plah-sah)(deh)(toh-rohs)* .... bullring
pluma, la *(ploo-mah)* .... pen
pobre *(poh-breh)* .... poor
poco *(poh-koh)* .... little, few
poder *(poh-dair)* .... to be able to, can
policía, la *(poh-lee-see-ah)* .... police (dept.)
política, la *(poh-lee-tee-kah)* .... politics
pollo, el *(poh-yoh)* .... *chicken*
Polo Norte, el *(poh-loh)(nor-teh)* .... North Pole
Polo Sur, el *(poh-loh)(soor)* .... South Pole
por *(por)* .... for, by, in
por favor *(por)(fah-vor)* .... please
por la mañana *(por)(lah)(mahn-yah-nah)* ... in the morning
por la tarde *(por)(lah)(tar-deh)* .... in the afternoon
¿por qué? *(por)(keh)* .... why?
portero, el *(por-teh-roh)* .... porter
Portugal *(por-too-gahl)* .... Portugal
portugués, el *(por-too-gwehs)* .... Portuguese
posible *(poh-see-bleh)* .... possible
práctica, la *(prahk-tee-kah)* .... practice
precio, el *(preh-see-oh)* .... price
precio del cuarto, el *(preh-see-oh)(del)(kwar-toh)* .....
.... price of the room
preciso *(preh-see-soh)* .... precious
predicción, la *(preh-deek-see-ohn)* .... prediction
prefacio, el *(preh-fah-see-oh)* .... preface
preferir *(preh-feh-reer)* .... to prefer
pregunta, la *(preh-goon-tah)* .... question
preparar *(preh-pah-rar)* .... to prepare
presente *(preh-sen-teh)* .... present
primavera, la *(pree-mah-veh-rah)* .... spring
primer piso, el *(pree-mair)(pee-soh)* .... first floor
principal *(preen-see-pahl)* .... principal, main
probable *(proh-bah-bleh)* .... probable
problema, el *(proh-bleh-mah)* .... problem
producto, el *(proh-dook-toh)* .... product
profesor, el *(proh-feh-sor)* .... professor
programa, el *(proh-grah-mah)* .... program
prohibido/a *(proh-hee-bee-doh)* .... prohibited
promesa, la *(proh-meh-sah)* .... promise
pronunciación, la *(proh-noon-see-ah-see-ohn)* .. pronunciation
propina, la *(proh-pee-nah)* .... tip
protestante *(proh-tes-tahn-teh)* .... Protestant
público/a *(poo-blee-koh)* .... public
puerta, la *(pwair-tah)* .... door
puerta de entrada, la *(pwair-tah)(deh)(en-trah-dah)* .. entrance
punto, el *(poon-toh)* .... point
punto de vista, el *(poon-toh)(deh)(vees-tah)* ...... viewpoint
púrpura *(poor-poo-rah)* .... purple

Q

¿qué? *(keh)* .... what?
¡Que aproveche! *(keh)(ah-proh-veh-cheh)* .. enjoy your meal!
¿Qué decimos? *(keh)(deh-see-mohs)* ...... what do we say?
¿Qué hora es? *(keh)(oh-rah)(es)* .... what time is it?
¿Qué hora tiene usted? *(keh)(oh-rah)(tee-en-eh)(oos-ted)* ...
.... what time do you have?
¿Qué necesita usted? *(keh)(neh-seh-see-tah)(oos-ted)* ......
.... what do you need?
¿Qué pasa? *(keh)(pah-sah)* .... what's happening?
¿Qué talla? *(keh)(tah-yah)* .... what size?

¿Qué tiempo hace hoy? *(keh)(tee-em-poh)(ah-seh)* . . . .
. . . . how is the weather today?
querer *(keh-rair)* . . . . to want
queso, el *(keh-soh)* . . . . cheese
¿quién? *(kee-en)* . . . . who?
¿Quién es? *(kee-en)(es)* . . . . who is it?
quince *(keen-seh)* . . . . fifteen
quinientos *(kee-nee-en-tohs)* . . . . five hundred

R

radio, la *(rah-dee-oh)* . . . . radio
ranchero, el *(rahn-cheh-roh)* . . . . rancher, farmer
rápido/a *(rah-pee-doh)* . . . . rapid
reacción, la *(reh-ahk-see-ohn)* . . . . reaction
rebelión, la *(reh-beh-lee-ohn)* . . . . rebellion
recibir *(reh-see-beer)* . . . . to receive
reclamación de maletas, la *(reh-klah-mah-see-hn)(deh)(mah-leh-tahs)* . . . . baggage claim
recuerdo, el *(reh-kwair-doh)* . . . . souvenir
refrigerador, el *(reh-free-heh-rah-dor)* . . . . refrigerator
regular *(reh-goo-lar)* . . . . regular
relación, la *(reh-lah-see-ohn)* . . . . relation
religión, la *(reh-lee-hee-ohn)* . . . . religion
reloj, el *(reh-loh)* . . . . clock, watch
relojería, la *(reh-loh-heh-ree-ah)* . . . . watchmaker's shop
remite, el *(reh-mee-teh)* . . . . return address
reparar *(reh-pah-rar)* . . . . to repair
repetir *(reh-peh-teer)* . . . . to repeat
¡repita por favor! *(reh-pee-tah)(por)(fah-vor)* repeat please!
república, la *(reh-poo-blee-kah)* . . . . republic
reserva, la *(reh-sair-vah)* . . . . reservation
reservación, la *(reh-sair-vah-see-ohn)* . . . . reservation
respuesta, la *(res-pwehs-tah)* . . . . answer
restaurante, el *(res-tow-rahn-teh)* . . . . restaurant
revista, la *(reh-vees-tah)* . . . . magazine
revolución, la *(reh-voh-loo-see-ohn)* . . . . revolution
rico/a *(ree-koh)* . . . . rich
rincón, el *(reen-kohn)* . . . . corner
rojo/a *(roh-hoh)* . . . . red
rollo de película, el *(roh-yoh)(deh)(peh-lee-koo-lah)* . . . .
. . . . roll of film
romano/a *(roh-mah-noh)* . . . . Roman
romántico/a *(roh-mahn-tee-koh)* . . . . romantic
ropa, la *(roh-pah)* . . . . clothes
ropero, el *(roh-peh-roh)* . . . . clothes closet
rosado/a *(roh-sah-doh)* . . . . pink
ruso, el *(roo-soh)* . . . . Russian

S

sábado, el *(sah-bah-doh)* . . . . Saturday
saber *(sah-bair)* . . . . to know
sal, la *(sahl)* . . . . salt
sala, la *(sah-lah)* . . . . living room
sala de espera, la *(sah-lah)(deh)(es-pair-ah)* . . waiting room
salario, el *(sah-lah-ree-oh)* . . . . salary
salida, la *(sah-lee-dah)* . . . . departure, exit
salida de urgencia, la *(sah-lee-dah)(deh)(oor-hen-see-ah)* . .
. . . . emergency exit
salir *(sah-leer)* . . . . to leave
salmón, el *(sahl-mohn)* . . . . salmon
sandalias, las *(sahn-dah-lee-ahs)* . . . . sandals
sano *(sah-noh)* . . . . healthy
santo, el *(sahn-toh)* . . . . saint
sardina, la *(sar-dee-nah)* . . . . sardine
sección de no fumar, la *(sek-see-ohn)(deh)(noh)(foo-mar)* . .
. . . . no smoking section
secretario, el *(seh-kreh-tah-ree-oh)* . . . . secretary
segundo, el *(seh-goon-doh)* . . . . second (unit of time)
segundo/a *(seh-goon-doh)* . . . . second
seis *(sehs)* . . . . six
seis mil *(sehs)(meel)* . . . . six thousand
sello, el *(say-yoh)* . . . . stamp
sellos de correo aéreo *(say-yohs)(deh)(koh-rreh-oh)(ah-eh-reh-oh)* . . . . airmail stamps

semana, la *(seh-mah-nah)* . . . . week
sensación, la *(sen-sah-see-ohn)* . . . . sensation
sentado/a *(sen-tah-doh)* . . . . seated
septiembre *(sep-tee-em-breh)* . . . . September
servicio, el *(sair-vee-see-oh)* . . . . service
servicios, los *(sair-vee-see-ohs)* . . . . restrooms
servilleta, la *(sair-vee-yeh-tah)* . . . . napkin
sesenta *(seh-sen-tah)* . . . . sixty
sesión, la *(seh-see-ohn)* . . . . session
setenta *(seh-ten-tah)* . . . . seventy
severo/a *(seh-veh-roh)* . . . . severe
sí *(see)* . . . . yes
sidra, la *(see-drah)* . . . . cider
siesta, la *(see-es-tah)* . . . . afternoon nap, quiet time
siete *(see-eh-teh)* . . . . seven
siete mil *(see-eh-teh)(meel)* . . . . seven thousand
siguiente *(see-gee-en-teh)* . . . . following
silencio, el *(see-len-see-oh)* . . . . silence
silla, la *(see-yah)* . . . . chair
simple *(seem-pleh)* . . . . simple
simultáneo/a *(see-mool-tah-neh-oh)* . . . . simultaneous
sinfonía, la *(seen-for-nee-ah)* . . . . symphony
sistema, el *(sees-teh-mah)* . . . . system
sobre *(soh-breh)* . . . . on top of, above, on
social *(soh-see-ahl)* . . . . social
sofá, el *(soh-fah)* . . . . sofa
sólido *(soh-lee-doh)* . . . . solid
solitario/a *(soh-lee-tah-ree-oh)* . . . . solitary
sombrero, el *(sohm-breh-roh)* . . . . hat
son *(sohn)* . . . . (they) are
son las cinco *(sohn)(lahs)(seen-koh)* . . . . it is five o'clock
sopa, la *(soh-pah)* . . . . soup
sostén, el *(sohs-ten)* . . . . bra
sótano, el *(soh-tah-noh)* . . . . basement
soy *(soy)* . . . . (I) am
su *(soo)* . . . . your, his, her, its, their
sudamericano/a *(sood-ah-meh-ree-kah-noh)* . . South American
suéter, el *(sweh-tair)* . . . . sweater
Suiza *(swee-sah)* . . . . Switzerland
sur, el *(soor)* . . . . south

T

tabaco, el *(tah-bah-koh)* . . . . tobacco
tabaquería, la *(tah-bah-keh-ree-ah)* . . . . tobacco shop
taberna, la *(tah-bair-nah)* . . . . bar
tablero, el *(tah-blair-oh)* . . . . counter
también *(tahm-bee-en)* . . . . also
tapas, las *(tah-pahs)* . . . . snacks
tarde, la *(tar-deh)* . . . . afternoon, evening
tarifa, la *(tah-fee-fah)* . . . . tariff
tarjeta postal, la *(tar-heh-tah)(pohs-tahl)* . . . . postcard
tarjetas de crédito, las *(tar-heh-tahs)(deh)(kreh-dee-toh)* . . .
. . . . credit cards
taxi, el *(tahk-see)* . . . . taxi
taza, la *(tah-sah)* . . . . cup
té, el *(the)* . . . . tea
té con leche, el *(teh)(kohn)(leh-cheh)* . . . . tea with milk
té con limón, el *(teh)(kohn)(lee-mohn)* . . . . . . tea with lemon
teatro, el *(teh-ah-troh)* . . . . theater
técnico/a *(tek-nee-koh)* . . . . technical
teléfono, el *(teh-leh-foh-noh)* . . . . telephone
teléfono público, el *(teh-leh-foh-noh)(poo-blee-koh)* . . . .
. . . . public telephone
telegrama, el *(teh-leh-grah-mah)* . . . . telegram
televisión, la *(teh-leh-vee-see-ohn)* . . . . television
televisor, el *(teh-leh-vee-sor)* . . . . television
temperatura, la *(tem-peh-rah-too-rah)* . . . . . . temperature
tenedor, el *(teh-neh-dor)* . . . . fork
tener *(teh-nair)* . . . . to have
tener que *(teh-nair)(keh)* . . . . to have to
tengo hambre *(tehn-goh)(ahm-breh)* . . . . I am hungry
tengo sed *(tehn-goh)(sed)* . . . . I am thirsty
terminal *(tair-mee-nahl)* . . . . terminal
termómetro, el *(tair-moh-meh-troh)* . . . . thermometer

ternera, la *(tair-neh-rah)* . . . . calf, veal
tía, la *(tee-ah)* . . . . aunt
tiempo, el *(tee-em-poh)* . . . . time, weather
tienda, la *(tee-en-dah)* . . . . store, shop
tienda de cámaras, la *(tee-en-dah)(deh)(kah-mah-rahs)* . . . .
. . . . camera store
tienda de comestibles, la *(tee-en-dah)(deh)(koh-mes-tee-bles)*
. . . . grocery store
tienda de ultramarinos, la *(tee-en-dah)(deh)(ool-trah-mah-*
ree-nohs) . . . . delicatessen
¿tiene usted? *(tee-en-eh)(oos-ted)* . . . . do you have?
tintorería, la *(teen-toh-reh-ree-ah)* . . . . dry cleaner's
tío, el *(tee-oh)* . . . . uncle
típico/a *(tee-pee-koh)* . . . . typical
tirar *(tee-rar)* . . . . pull (doors)
toalla, la *(toh-ah-yah)* . . . . towel
todo/a *(toh-doh)* . . . . all, everything
Todos los Santos, los *(toh-dohs)(lohs)(sahn-tohs)* . . . .
. . . . All Saint's Day
tomate, el *(toh-mah-teh)* . . . . tomato
tortilla, la *(tor-tee-yah)* . . . . omelette
total *(toh-tahl)* . . . . total
trágico/a *(trah-hee-koh)* . . . . tragic
traje, el *(trah-heh)* . . . . suit
traje de baño, el *(trah-heh)(deh)(bahn-yoh)* . . . . swimsuit
tranquilo/a *(trahn-kee-loh)* . . . . tranquil, quiet
transparente *(trahns-pah-ren-teh)* . . . . transparent
transportar *(trahns-por-tar)* . . . . to transport
tranvía, el *(trahn-vee-ah)* . . . . streetcar
trece *(treh-seh)* . . . . thirteen
treinta *(train-tah)* . . . . thirty
tren, el *(tren)* . . . . train
tren correo, el *(tren)(koh-rreh-oh)* . . . . mail train (slow)
tren expresso, el *(tren)(ek-spreh-soh)* . . . . express train
tren rápido, el *(tren)(rah-pee-doh)* . . . . fast train
tres *(trehs)* . . . . three
tres mil *(trehs)(meel)* . . . . three thousand
triángulo, el *(tree-ahn-goo-loh)* . . . . triangle
triunfante *(tree-oon-fahn-teh)* . . . . triumphant
trivial *(tree-vee-ahl)* . . . . trivial
trolebús, el *(troh-leh-boos)* . . . . trolleybus
trompeta, la *(trohm-peh-tah)* . . . . trumpet
tropical *(troh-pee-kahl)* . . . . tropical
tú *(too)* . . . . you (singular, informal)
tumulto, el *(too-mool-toh)* . . . . tumult
túnel, el *(too-nel)* . . . . tunnel
turista, el *(too-rees-tah)* . . . . tourist
tutor, el *(too-tor)* . . . . tutor

U

último/a *(ool-tee-moh)* . . . . ultimate, last
un *(oon)* . . . . a/an (masculine singular)
un momento *(oon)(moh-men-toh)* . . . . just a minute
una *(oon-ah)* . . . . a/an (feminine singular)
unas *(oon-ahs)* . . . . some (feminine plural)
unos *(oon-ohs))* . . . . some (masculine plural or mixed)
uniforme, el *(oo-nee-for-meh)* . . . . uniform
unión, la *(oo-nee-ohn)* . . . . union
universidad, la *(oo-nee-vair-see-dahd)* . . . . university
uno *(oon-oh)* . . . . one
urbano/a *(oor-bah-noh)* . . . . urban
urgente *(oor-heh-teh)* . . . . urgent
usar *(oo-sar)* . . . . to use
usted *(oos-ted) abbre. Ud.* . . . . you (singular, formal)
ustedes *(oos-teh-des) abbre. Uds.* . . . . . . you (plural, formal)
usual *(oo-soo-ahl)* . . . . usual
utensilio, el *(oo-ten-see-leh-oh)* . . . . utensil
utilidad, la *(oo-tee-lee-dahd)* . . . . utility

V

vaca, la *(vah-kah)* . . . . cow
vacaciones, las *(vah-kah-see-oh-nes)* . . . . vacation
vacante, la *(vah-kahn-teh)* . . . . vacant

vagabundo, el *(vah-gah-boon-doh)* . . . . vagabond
vainilla, la *(vy-nee-yah)* . . . . vanilla
válido/a *(vah-lee-doh)* . . . . valid
valle, el *(vah-yeh)* . . . . valley
vanidad, la *(vah-nee-dahd)* . . . . vanity
vaqueros, los *(vah-key-rohs)* . . . . blue jeans
variedad, la *(vah-ree-eh-dahd)* . . . . variety
varios/as *(vah-ree-ohs)* . . . . various
vaso, el *(vah-soh)* . . . . glass (to drink from)
vaso para vino, el *(vah-soh)(pah-rah)(vee-noh)* . . . wine glass
Vaticano, el *(vah-tee-kah-noh)* . . . . the Vatican
vehículo, el *(veh-hee-koo-loh)* . . . . vehicle
veinte *(vain-teh)* . . . . twenty
vender *(ven-dair)* . . . . to sell
Venezuela *(ven-es-weh-lah)* . . . . Venezuela
venir *(veh-neer)* . . . . to come
ventana, la *(ven-tah-nah)* . . . . window
ventanilla, la *(ven-tah-nee-yah)* . . . . ticket counter, window
ver *(vair)* . . . . to see
verano, el *(veh-rah-noh)* . . . . summer
verbo, el *(vair-boh)* . . . . verb
verde *(vair-deh)* . . . . green
verdulería, la *(vair-doo-leh-ree-ah)* . . . .
. . . . vegetable store, greengrocer's
vestido, el *(ves-tee-doh)* . . . . dress
viajar *(vee-ah-har)* . . . . to travel
viajar en coche *(vee-ah-har)(en)(koh-cheh)* . to travel by car
viaje, el *(vee-ah-heh)* . . . . trip, journey
viajero, el *(vee-ah-heh-roh)* . . . . traveler
viejo/a *(vee-eh-hoh)* . . . . old
viento *(vee-en-toh)* . . . . wind
viernes *(vee-air-nes)* . . . . Friday
Viernes Santo *(vee-air-nes)(sahn-toh)* . . . . Good Friday
vinagre, el *(vee-nah-greh)* . . . . vinegar
vino, el *(vee-noh)* . . . . wine
violeta *(vee-oh-leh-tah)* . . . . violet (color)
violín, el *(vee-oh-leen)* . . . . violin
visa, la *(vee-sah)* . . . . visa
visita, la *(vee-see-tah)* . . . . visit
visitar *(vee-see-tar)* . . . . to visit
vivir *(vee-veer)* . . . . to live
volar *(voh-lar)* . . . . to fly
vosotros *(voh-soh-trohs)* . . . . you (plural, informal)
vuelo, el *(vweh-loh)* . . . . flight

Y

y *(ee)* . . . . and
y cuarto *(ee)(kwar-toh)* . . . . quarter after (time)
y media *(ee)(meh-dee-ah)* . . . . half past (time)
yo *(yoh)* I
yo necesito *(yoh)(neh-seh-see-toh)* . . . . I need
yo quiero *(yoh)(kee-eh-roh))* . . . . I want
yo quisiera una reservación *(yoh)(kee-see-eh-rah)(oon-ah)*
(reh-sair-vah-see-ohn) . . . . I would like a reservation
yo soy *(yoh)(soy)* . . . . I am

Z

zapatillas, las *(sah-pah-tee-yahs)* . . . . slippers
zapatos, los *(sah-pah-tohs)* . . . . shoes
zapatos de tenis, los *(sah-pah-tohs)(deh)(teh-nees)* . . . .
. . . . tennis shoes
zodíaco, el *(soh-dee-ah-koh)* . . . . zodiac
zona, la *(soh-nah)* . . . . zone
zoología, la *(soh-oh-loh-hee-ah)* . . . . zoology
zoológico *(soh-oh-loh-hee-koh)* . . . . zoological

Did you have fun learning your new language?
We at Bilingual Books hope you enjoy your
travels wherever they might take you!

This beverage guide is intended to explain the variety of beverages available to you while **en México o** any other Spanish-speaking country. It is by no means complete. Some of the experimenting has been left up to you, but this should get you started.

BEBIDAS CALIENTES (hot drinks)

café	coffee
café con leche	coffee with milk
café americano	American-style coffee
café corto	espresso
café cortado	capuccino
chocolate	cocoa

té	tea
té con limón	tea with lemon
té con leche	tea with milk

BEBIDAS FRÍAS (cold drinks)

leche	milk
batido	milkshake
jugo/zumo	juice
jugo de naranja	orange juice
jugo de tomate	tomato juice
agua	water
agua mineral	mineral water
agua gaseosa	club soda
agua tónica	tonic water
sidra	cider
hielo	ice

VINOS (wine)

There are four main types of **vino**, but quality levels vary drastically. **Vino** can be purchased by the **botella** (bottle) or by the **vaso** (glass).

vino tinto	red wine
vino blanco	white wine
vino rosado	rosé wine
clarete	light red wine
vino corriente/común ..	ordinary table wine
vino reserva	"reserved," aged wine
vino dulce	sweet wine
vino seco	dry wine
champaña	champagne
jerez	sherry
sangría	wine drink made with fruits, brandy, lemonade and ice

CERVEZAS (beer)

There are many brands of beer. **Cerveza** is generally purchased by the **botella** (bottle) or **de barril** (draught).

BEBIDAS ALCOHÓLICAS (alcohol)

vodka	vodka
whisky	whisky
whisky escocés	scotch
whisky borbón	bourbon
ginebra	gin
ron	rum
coñac	cognac
aperitivo	aperitif
licor	liqueur

La Carta
menu

CUT ALONG DOTTED LINE, FOLD AND TAKE WITH YOU

FOLD HERE

FOLD HERE

Método de Preparación

a la Romana	in batter
cocido	cooked, broiled
frito	fried
al horno	baked
cocido al vapor	steamed
a la parrilla	grilled
a la plancha	grilled, broiled
empanado	breaded
salteado	sautéed
asado	roasted
crudo	raw
medio crudo	rare
en su punto	medium
bien asado	well-done

General

conserva	jam
mermelada	marmalade
miel	honey
sal	salt
pimienta	pepper
aceite	oil
vinagre	vinegar
mostaza	mustard
salsa	sauce
queso	cheese
ajo	garlic
torta	cake
pastel	pastry
helado	ice cream
nata, crema batida	whipped cream
postre	dessert
flan	caramel custard

Fruta (fruit)

manzana	apple
pera	pear
albaricoque	apricot
melocotón, durazno	peach
plátano	banana
naranja	orange
cereza	cherry
ciruela	plum
toronja/pomelo	grapefruit
uvas	grapes
limón	lemon
piña	pineapple
melón	melon
sandía	watermelon
guayaba	guava
fresas/frutillas	strawberries
frambuesas	raspberries
mirtillos	bilberries
zarzamoras	blackberries
macedonia de fruta	fruit cocktail
compota de manzana	applesauce

Bebidas (beverages)

cerveza	beer
leche	milk
café	coffee
café con leche	coffee with milk
zumo de …	juice of …
jugo de …	juice of …
limonada	lemonade
agua mineral	bottled water
vino tinto	red wine
vino blanco	white wine
vino rosado	rosé wine

(keh) *(ah-proh-veh-cheh)*
¡Que aproveche!
enjoy your meal

Pan y Pasta (bread and pasta)

pan	bread
panecillo	roll
pan moreno	dark (rye) bread
pan tostado	toast
arroz	rice
macarrones	macaroni
espagueti	spaghetti

Legumbres (vegetables)

guisantes	peas
espárragos	asparagus
alcachofas	artichokes
zanahorias	carrots
berenjena	eggplant
judías verdes	green beans
espinaca	spinach
batatas	sweet potatoes
champiñones	mushrooms
coliflor	cauliflower
maíz	corn
cebollas	onions
rábanos	radishes
remolachas	beets
lentejas	lentils
frijoles	kidney beans

Patatas/Papas (potatoes)

patatas cocidas	boiled potatoes
patatas al horno	baked potatoes
puré de patatas	mashed potatoes
patatas fritas	French fried potatoes
patatas rellenas	stuffed potatoes
patatas a la vasca	potatoes with garlic, olive oil and clove

Salchichas (sausages)

salchichón	salami
chorizo	garlic-spiced sausage
mortadela	pork sausage
tocino	bacon
jamón	ham

Entremeses (hors d'oeuvres)

ostras/ostiones	oysters
coctel de langosta	lobster cocktail
coctel de mariscos	seafood cocktail
arenque ahumado	smoked herring
caviar	caviar
caracoles	snails
ensaladilla rusa	Russian eggs
fiambres	cold cuts
almejas al natural	clams
jamón serrano	smoked ham
paella	saffron rice with seafood, meat and vegetables

Sopas (soups)

gazpacho	cold tomato soup
consomé/caldo	consommé/broth
sopa de fideos	noodle soup
sopa de pollo	chicken soup
sopa al jerez	beef broth with sherry
crema de champiñones	cream-of-mushroom soup
crema reina	cream-of-chicken soup
sopa al queso	cheese soup
menestra	stew
cocido español	thick meat soup

Huevos (eggs)

huevos duros	hard-cooked eggs
huevos pasados por agua	soft-boiled eggs
huevos fritos	fried eggs
huevos revueltos	scrambled eggs
huevos escalfados	poached eggs
tortilla de . . .	omelette with . . .
suflé	soufflé

Carne (meat)

Ternera (veal)

ternera asada	roast veal
ternera borracha	veal strips in white wine
ternera en adobo	marinated veal
ternera rellena	stuffed veal

FOLD HERE

Vaca (beef)

filete	filet
entrecote	boneless rib steak
solomillo	sirloin
tournedos	tenderloin
biftec	steak
rosbif	roast beef
chuletas de res	prime ribs
churrasco	charcoal-grilled meat
albóndigas	meat balls
hígado	liver
lengua	tongue

Cerdo (pork)

lomo de cerdo	pork loin
chuletas de cerdo	pork chops
lomo relleno	stuffed pork loin
cerdo asado	pork roast
filete de cerdo	pork tenderloin
asado de cerdo	roast pork
costillas de cerdo	spareribs
cochinillo asado	roast suckling pig
jamón	ham

Cordero (lamb)

chuletas de cordero	lamb chops
pierna de cordero	leg of lamb
cordero asado	roast lamb
cordero estofado	casserole of stuffed lamb
brochetas de filete	shish kebab

FOLD HERE

Aves y Caza (poultry and game)

pollo	chicken
pato	duck
pavo	turkey
pollo asado	roast chicken
pollo a la cazuela	chicken casserole
pollo al jerez	chicken in sherry
liebre	hare
conejo	rabbit
faisán	pheasant
perdiz	partridge
codorniz	quail
venado	venison

Pescado y Mariscos (fish and seafood)

trucha	trout
lenguado	sole
bacalao	cod
platija	flounder
merluza	hake
arenque	herring
pargo	snapper
atún	tuna
cangrejo	crab
calamares	squid
gambas	prawns
camarones	shrimp
mejillones	mussels

Ensaladas (salads)

ensalada de lechuga	lettuce salad
ensalada de frutas	fruit salad
ensalada de legumbres	vegetable salad
ensalada de tomates	tomato salad
ensalada de patatas	potato salad
ensalada de pepinos	cucumber salad
ensalada mixta	mixed salad
ensalada del tiempo	seasonal salad
ensalada corriente	seasonal salad
ensalada de pollo	chicken salad
ensalada remolacha	red beet salad

(The following items appear in the Entremeses/Vaca column between Vaca and Aves y Caza section)

biftec de ternera	veal steak
escalope de ternera	veal cutlet
chuletas de ternera	veal chops
escalopes Vienesa	breaded cutlet with anchovy butter
escalopes Milanesa	breaded cutlet with egg and cheese
escalopes cordon bleu	veal stuffed with ham and cheese
ternera al jerez	veal in sherry
ternera jardinera	veal with vegetables
riñones	kidneys

(yoh) **yo**	*(noh-soh-trohs)* **nosotros**
(el) **él**	*(oos-ted)* **usted**
(eh-yah) **ella**	*(eh-yohs)* *(eh-yahs)* **ellos/ellas**
(neh-seh-see-tar) **necesitar** *(neh-seh-see-toh)* **yo necesito**	*(ahn-dar)* **andar** *(ahn-doh)* **yo ando**
(ah-pren-dair) **aprender** *(ah-pren-doh)* **yo aprendo**	*(veh-neer)* **venir** *(vehn-goh)* **yo vengo**
(teh-nair) **tener** *(tehn-goh)* **yo tengo**	*(keh-rair)* **querer** *(kee-eh-roh)* **yo quiero**

we	I
you	he
they (♂) / they (♀)	she
to walk/go	to need
I walk/go	I need
to come	to learn
I come	I learn
to want	to have
I want	I have

(kohm-prar)
comprar
(kohm-proh)
yo compro

(ah-blar)
hablar
(ah-bloh)
yo hablo

(vee-veer)
vivir
(vee-voh)
yo vivo

(peh-deer)
pedir
(pee-doh)
yo pido

(en-trar)
entrar
(en-troh)
yo entro

(deh-seer)
decir
(dee-goh)
yo digo

(koh-mair)
comer
(koh-moh)
yo como

(beh-bair)
beber
(beh-boh)
yo bebo

(meh)   *(yah-moh)*
me llamo . . .

(en-kohn-trar)
encontrar
(en-kwen-troh)
yo encuentro

(kohm-pren-dair)
comprender
(kohm-pren-doh)
yo comprendo

(reh-peh-teer)
repetir
(reh-pee-toh)
yo repito

to speak	to buy
I speak	I buy
to order/request	to live
I order/request	I live
to say	to enter
I say	I enter
to drink	to eat
I drink	I eat
to find	my name is . . .
I find	
to repeat	to understand
I repeat	I understand

(ven-dair)
vender
(ven-doh)
yo vendo

(vair)
ver
(veh-oh)
yo veo

(mahn-dar)
mandar
(mahn-doh)
yo mando

(dor-meer)
dormir
(dwair-moh)
yo duermo

(yah-mar)
llamar
(yah-moh)
yo llamo

(ah-sair)
hacer
(ah-goh)
yo hago

(dah-meh)
Dame . . .

(es-kree-beer)
escribir
(es-kree-boh)
yo escribo

(pah-gar)
pagar
(pah-goh)
yo pago

(poh-dair)
poder
(pweh-doh)
yo puedo

(teh-nair)   *(keh)*
tener que
(tehn-goh)   *(keh)*
yo tengo que

(sah-bair)
saber
(say)
yo sé

to see	to sell
I see	I sell
to sleep	to send
I sleep	I send
to make/do	to call
I make/do	I call
to write	
I write	Give me . . .
to be able to/can	to pay
I can	I pay
to know (fact)	to have to/must
I know	I have to/must

(leh-air)
leer

(leh-oh)
yo leo

(voh-lar)
volar

(vweh-loh)
yo vuelo

(vee-ah-har)
viajar

(vee-ah-hoh)
yo viajo

(sah-leer)
salir

(sahl-goh)
yo salgo

(yeh-gar)
llegar

(yeh-goh)
yo llego

(kahm-bee-ar)
cambiar

(kahm-bee-oh)
yo cambio

(ah-sair) *(lah)* *(mah-leh-tah)*
hacer la maleta

(ah-goh) *(mah-leh-tah)*
yo hago la maleta

(eer)
ir

(voy)
yo voy

(ah-ee)
hay

(tee-en-eh) *(oos-ted)*
Tiene usted . . .

(par-teer)
partir

(ow-toh-boos) *(par-teh)*
el autobús parte

(eer) *(koh-cheh)*
ir en coche

(voy) *(koh-cheh)*
yo voy en coche

to fly	to read
I fly	I read
to leave/exit	to travel
I leave/exit	I travel
to transfer (vehicles) /to change money	to arrive
I transfer/change money	I arrive
to go/drive	to pack
I go/drive	I pack
Do you have . . .	there is/there are
to drive	to depart (vehicles)
I drive	the bus departs

(oy)
hoy

(koh-moh) *(es-tah)* *(oos-ted)*
¿Cómo está usted?

(ah-yair)
ayer

(por) *(fah-vor)*
por favor

(mahn-yah-nah)
mañana

(grah-see-ahs)
gracias

(ah-dee-ohs)
adiós

(pair-doh-neh-meh)
perdóneme

(vee-eh-hoh) *(nweh-voh)*
viejo - nuevo

(kwahn-toh) *(kwes-tah)*
¿Cuánto cuesta?

(grahn-deh) *(peh-kehn-yoh)*
grande - pequeño

(ah-bee-air-toh) *(seh-rrah-doh)*
abierto - cerrado

How are you?	today
please	yesterday
thank you	tomorrow
excuse me	good-bye
How much does this cost?	old - new
open - closed	large - small

(en-fair-moh)   *(sah-noh)*

enfermo - sano

(bweh-noh)   *(mah-loh)*

bueno - malo

(kah-lee-en-teh)   *(free-oh)*

caliente - frío

(kor-toh)   *(lar-goh)*

corto - largo

(ahl-toh)   *(bah-hoh)*

alto - bajo

(ah-rree-bah)   *(ah-bah-hoh)*

arriba - abajo

(ees-kee-air-dah)   *(deh-reh-chah)*

izquierda - derecha

(rah-pee-doh)   *(des-pah-see-oh)*

rápido - despacio

(vee-eh-hoh)   *(hoh-ven)*

viejo - joven

(bah-rah-toh)   *(kah-roh)*

barato - caro

(poh-breh)   *(ree-koh)*

pobre - rico

(moo-choh)   *(poh-koh)*

mucho - poco

good - bad	ill - healthy
short - long	hot - cold
above - below	high - low
fast - slow	left - right
inexpensive - expensive	old - young
a lot - a little	poor - rich

Now that you've finished...

You've done it!

You've completed all the Steps, stuck your labels, flashed your cards, cut out your beverage and menu guides and practiced your new language. Do you realize how far you've come and how much you've learned? You've accomplished what it could take years to achieve in a traditional language class.

You can now confidently

- ask questions,
- understand directions,
- make reservations,
- order food and
- shop for anything.

And you can do it all in a foreign language! Go anywhere with confidence — from a large cosmopolitan restaurant to a small, out-of-the-way village where no one speaks English. Your experiences will be much more enjoyable and worry-free now that you speak the language.

As you've seen, learning a foreign language can be fun. Why limit yourself to just one? Now you're ready to learn another language with the *10 minutes a day*® Series!

Kris Kershul

Kristine Kershul

To place an order –

- Visit us at www.bbks.com, day or night.

- Call us at (800) 488-5068 or (206) 284-4211 between 8:00 a.m. and 5:00 p.m. Pacific Time, Monday - Friday.

- If you have questions about ordering, please call us. You may also fax us at (206) 284-3660 or email us at customer.service@bbks.com.